A *Word From*
Stephen Paul Mahinka
Morgan Lewis

We are pleased to be a part of this important new book, *Inside the Minds: Winning Antitrust Strategies*, published by Aspatore Books. Competitive strategies and competitor and government challenges have made a working knowledge of antitrust more important in recent years than ever before for senior corporate executives. We have long had at Morgan Lewis one of the largest and most sophisticated international antitrust practices in the world, helping executives to deal in a practical way with all of the difficult areas covered by this volume. We hope you both learn from and enjoy the book.

Praise for *Inside the Minds*

"Unlike any other business book." - Bruce Keller, Partner, Debevoise & Plimpton

"The *Inside the Minds* series is a valuable probe into the thought, perspectives, and techniques of accomplished professionals. By taking a 50,000 foot view, the authors place their endeavors in a context rarely gleaned from text books or treatise." - Chuck Birenbaum, Partner, Thelen Reid & Priest

"A snapshot of everything you need..." - Charles Koob, Co-Head of Litigation Department, Simpson Thacher & Bartlet

"Tremendous insights..." - James Quinn, Litigation Chair, Weil Gotshal & Manges

"A rare peek behind the curtains and into the minds of the industry's best." - Brandon Baum, Partner, Cooley Godward

"Intensely personal, practical advice from seasoned dealmakers." - Mary Ann Jorgenson, Coordinator of Business Practice Area, Squire, Sanders & Dempsey

"An informative insider's perspective." - Gary Klotz, Labor & Employment Law Practice Group Manager, Butzel Long

"Great practical advice and thoughtful insights." - Mark Gruhin, Partner, Schmeltzer, Aptaker & Shepard, P.C.

About *Inside the Minds*

The critically acclaimed *Inside the Minds* series provides readers of all levels with proven business intelligence from C-Level executives (CEO, CFO, CTO, CMO, Partner) from the world's most respected companies. Each chapter is comparable to a white paper or essay and is a future-oriented look at where an industry/profession/topic is heading and the most important issues for future success. Each author has been carefully chosen through an exhaustive selection process by the *Inside the Minds* editorial board to write a chapter for this book. *Inside the Minds* was conceived in order to give readers actual insights into the leading minds of business executives worldwide. Because so few books or other publications are actually written by executives in industry, *Inside the Minds* presents an unprecedented look at various industries and professions never before available.

Inside the Minds:
Winning Antitrust Strategies

Leading Attorneys on Mastering the Laws that Regulate, Promote and Protect Competition

Published by Aspatore, Inc.

For corrections, company/title updates, comments or any other inquiries please email info@aspatore.com.

First Printing, 2004
10 9 8 7 6 5 4 3 2 1

ISBN 1-58762-438-9 Library of Congress Control Number: 2003099223

Inside the Minds Managing Editor, Carolyn Murphy, Edited by Michaela Falls, Proofread by Eddie Fournier, Cover design by Scott Rattray & Ian Mazie

Material in this book is for educational purposes only. This book is sold with the understanding that neither the authors nor the publisher are engaged in rendering medical, legal, accounting, investment, or any other professional service. For legal advice, please consult your personal lawyer.

This book is printed on acid free paper.

A special thanks to all the individuals who made this book possible.

The views expressed by the individuals in this book (or the individuals on the cover) do not necessarily reflect the views shared by the companies they are employed by (or the companies mentioned in this book). The employment status and affiliations of authors with the companies referenced are subject to change.

ABOUT ASPATORE BOOKS

www.Aspatore.com

Aspatore Books is the largest and most exclusive publisher of C-Level executives (CEO, CFO, CTO, CMO, Partner) from the world's most respected companies. Aspatore annually publishes C-Level executives from over half the Global 500, top 250 professional services firms, law firms (MPs/Chairs), and other leading companies of all sizes. By focusing on publishing only C-Level executives, Aspatore provides professionals of all levels with proven business intelligence from industry insiders, rather than relying on the knowledge of unknown authors and analysts. Aspatore is a privately held company headquartered in Boston, Massachusetts, with employees around the world.

Inside the Minds:
Winning Antitrust Strategies
Leading Attorneys on Mastering the Laws that Regulate, Promote and Protect Competition

CONTENTS

Applying Antitrust Law Effectively:

The Importance of Simplifying Complexity

Stephen Paul Mahinka

Manager, Antitrust Practice Group &
Chair, Life Sciences Interdisciplinary Group
Morgan, Lewis & Bockius LLP

The importance of obtaining effective antitrust advice and assistance has never been greater for business. Restructuring of industries deriving from numerous sources, including increased internationalization, deregulation, and more rapid evolution of the technological bases of competition, results in more merger, joint venture, and licensing activity. The internationalization of antitrust review by numerous national regulators also has increased the complexity of satisfying competition concerns. Further, the expansion of the range and types of antitrust litigation, particularly regarding cartels, pricing in several high profile industries such as pharmaceuticals, and by state attorneys general, has further increased the prominence of antitrust concerns. The explosion of data, readily available through the Internet, paradoxically adds to the difficulty of properly analyzing situations and providing practical and effective resolutions to competition issues.

All of these developments, and the continued evolution of antitrust analysis and its supporting economics, make simplifying complexity – the ability to understand the data and the dynamics of the industry and develop practical solutions – the overwhelming imperative today for the antitrust practitioner.

Essential Capabilities of the Antitrust Practitioner

An antitrust lawyer needs to have three skills. First, he or she has to have a very high level knowledge of antitrust, which includes both antitrust law and antitrust economics. Second, he or she needs to have knowledge of the company being represented, the regulatory and business environment in which the company operates, and the structure and dynamics of its market. Third, an antitrust lawyer must have the ability to integrate this knowledge and apply it with common sense, to give clear, helpful and practical suggestions and provide creative resolutions for transactions and litigation.

Seeing through complexity is the hallmark of an outstanding antitrust lawyer. It is easy to become overwhelmed by complicated facts and regulatory environments and simply advise the client that the risks are unmanageable. An effective antitrust lawyer needs to be able to see the way to creative solutions to complex problems in a complex environment.

To a large extent, developments in technology have altered the types of activity engaged in by antitrust lawyers. It used to be that clients would ask us to find information about their industry, how their industry was considered from a competition standpoint, whether there were prior cases which involved their industry, and the current views of the enforcement agencies. We often were asked to find speeches and comments that were recently given about their specific problem by relevant enforcement agencies. Now, clients can and do obtain all of that information themselves on the Internet. Clients simply do not ask us for that type of information anymore. Today, antitrust lawyers instead serve our clients by making sense of the incredibly voluminous amounts of material that they often have already obtained. The antitrust lawyer then organizes, analyzes, distills, simplifies and clarifies this information for the client, and provides proposed resolutions that are practical from a business standpoint.

Presently, the biggest problem for analysis is that there is more information available than people know what to do with. Therefore, while technology has increased our ability to obtain information, the amount of information available actually has made the analytical process more difficult. As a result, that makes "simplifying complexity" the hallmark of a great antitrust lawyer, to a greater degree than ever before.

The Benefits of a Mentor

There is no substitute in professional development for working with a great antitrust lawyer. It is extremely valuable for junior lawyers to be exposed to how a senior lawyer analyzes a problem, delivers the analysis, and constructs creative solutions. That is the best way to learn.

Miles W. Kirkpatrick founded our antitrust practice group three decades ago. He returned to the firm after having been Chair of the Federal Trade Commission, and his presence was the reason for me coming to Morgan Lewis. A few years later we had a very difficult case regarding predatory pricing that another law firm had lost in district court. The client came to our firm and asked us if we would take the case on appeal.

I spent a lot of time researching and reviewing the trial record, and came up with what I thought were some really good theories for the appeal. The case had been decided against our client based on an inference from certain indirect evidence. Miles looked at everything I had done and at what had gone on below in the trial court, and simply said, "It occurs to me that there is actual evidence here that there was no effect on pricing. Doesn't that trump all of the inferences and all the cases cited and record data, and isn't that the way to attack the judgment below?" He was absolutely correct, and his analysis ended up being accepted by the United States Court of Appeal for the Third Circuit. Significantly, it is still the legal standard for predatory pricing analysis today, twenty years later.

That is an example of how, if you know the antitrust field and the industry, and you have well-honed practical judgment, you can simplify your analysis to the point where you can say, "This is a way through all of this case analysis and facts and documents that have been produced below. And this is the way to present it." You learn that only by working with the best. It is something that you have to experience in process. You cannot simply be told what to do, because it doesn't mean anything until you see it generated by a great antitrust lawyer in a particular context.

Antitrust and Economic Policy and Analysis

Antitrust law is a fascinating way to become involved with public economic policy and analysis. I have always enjoyed the study of politics and economics and business history. In practicing antitrust, a lawyer is able to keep abreast of developments in economics and, in a small way, participate in the structuring of the future of the American economic system. I can see this participation in little ways every day, whether by working on distribution agreements or mergers, representing clients in antitrust litigation, or assisting in developing strategic responses to fundamental changes in an industry.

Antitrust analysis can be applied to any industry, so antitrust lawyers need not focus on just one industry. For example, insights that I glean from my work in past industry restructurings, such as natural gas, airlines, trucking, or cable television, are hugely useful in analyzing and advising on industry restructuring in other areas, such as life sciences and energy. Further, the knowledge of and facility with economic analysis that is a basic requirement for an effective antitrust lawyer is of immense utility in working with industries with complex and rapidly evolving economic structures, including life sciences/healthcare and energy at present.

Antitrust is also an area of the law that is always changing. The approach and base of knowledge of antitrust lawyers today is quite different from the analysis, economics, and approach used by antitrust lawyers in 1980. It is a fascinating way to stay involved with the immense changes that take place in American business.

Counseling the Client

When counseling a client, an antitrust lawyer must know the industry's structure, its dynamics, and its regulatory environment. For example, if you are involved in a pharmaceutical industry matter, you must understand the impact of the Food and Drug Administration (FDA) regulation on the process of new drug approvals, and of healthcare regulation that affects the pricing and reimbursement of products by the Centers for Medicare and Medicaid Services. You likely also will need to understand the effect and operation of the Waxman-Hatch Amendments to the food and drug laws regarding patent term extension and market exclusivity protections for drugs. You have to know the particular business and regulatory environment of your client. You simply cannot give antitrust advice in a vacuum and fail to take into account the specific context of the industry, which may radically alter conventional antitrust advice. Responding at such a high level of abstraction fails to give the practical assistance that the client needs.

It is also vitally important to make the complexity of antitrust understandable to the client. Antitrust lawyers can speak in a language that is fairly incomprehensible to our own clients, let alone others, who are not involved in the field. There are a lot of specialized terminology and concepts used in this area of the law, such as cross-elasticities of demand, game theoretic models, and market concentration indices, such as the Herfindahl-Hirschman Index. As an antitrust lawyer, you have to be able to translate the law for the client so that he or she understands it, and interpret the law so that the advice you provide is both helpful and practical.

Dealing with Regulatory Agencies

When representing a client involved in an industry that is subject to many regulators, antitrust lawyers must adapt and balance the story we are telling -- that the transaction is pro-competitive and efficiency enhancing -- to a variety of audiences. Some agencies look at competition issues much differently than others. For instance, in an energy industry merger, not only will the Federal Trade Commission or the Department of Justice Antitrust Division be involved, as likely will the Federal Energy Regulatory Commission, but state attorneys general from several states and state public utility commissions and their associated consumer advocates may also be involved. If there are nuclear units, the Nuclear Regulatory Commission may be relevant. The Securities and Exchange Commission may be involved, if the company is governed by the Public Utility Holding Company Act of 1935. Further, there may be foreign government agencies to deal with, since international operations may be involved.

To deal with all these agencies, the antitrust lawyer must balance and coordinate the competitive effects presentation. Sometimes, of course, simply answering just one regulatory agency can be a challenge. Having five or fifteen to respond to, and trying to decide how to balance and sequence the responses, is tougher. More significantly as an antitrust lawyer, you have to think about what concessions you are willing to make in order to get the deal through. What might be acceptable as a concession to one regulatory or enforcement agency may be totally meaningless to another. The ability to deal with multiple agencies and move the process along for a client is very challenging, requiring creativity, knowledge of the regulatory environment, and practical judgment.

Agency Investigations

Antitrust issues are more likely to arise in two kinds of industries: one is industries that deal in commodities, because such products are sold based on price. Steel beams, aluminum ingots, or bulk vitamins are examples of commodities where price is the only differentiating factor. There will always be a concern that there is price-fixing and price signaling in such industries and, as a result, antitrust issues can be expected to arise on a recurrent basis.

A second area where competition questions commonly can be expected to arise is in industries that are undergoing restructuring. When an industry is undergoing restructuring, its member companies may respond very differently. Some companies will sell off assets, restructure, and may become involved in other areas. Others will attempt to consolidate in the core industry area. As a result, all sorts of competition issues will arise due to the increase of mergers and acquisitions, joint ventures, licensing and other transactions. In addition, there will be new pricing and distribution issues, and other competitive disputes that will likely result in antitrust litigation.

Regardless of the source of competition concerns, the most important thing to do for a client that is facing questions about an activity or transaction is to let the client know that it is possible to respond effectively if it has a good business rationale for the challenged activity. I tell our clients that if what they are doing makes sense from a business perspective, if they have a good business justification for making the decision, then, nine times out of ten, that reason will be deemed pro-competitive. The agency reviewing the transaction or activity will likely conclude, "Yes, that enhances efficiency, that is pro-competitive, and that is allowable."

If a client can explain with clarity what it was thinking when it made its decision -- why it is proposing to do this joint venture, why it is asking to make this acquisition, why it undertook pricing in that way -- then it will probably be defensible from an antitrust perspective. In many cases, however, the client's decisions have not been clearly thought through. The role we play then is to pull together an explanation, to simplify and clarify what the business wants to do and why it is important to that business and that industry, so that a coherent and compelling legal and business rationale can be presented.

Risk: Making Sense of It for Clients

The best service an antitrust lawyer can provide is to give the client alternative solutions that are practical from a business standpoint. The easiest thing to say is, "You can't do that because it will create an antitrust issue." There is always going to be an antitrust risk. The conservative approach of just saying no is very tempting, because then you never have to go out on a limb as an antitrust lawyer. You will never be criticized, because nothing will ever happen. However, an antitrust lawyer who does that is not serving the client very well. When we are training our junior lawyers, we try to show them that the real service we provide is coming up with alternatives to risky transactions that still get our client as much as possible of what it wants. The best antitrust lawyers know the antitrust laws well enough, and know the industry and its structural environment and dynamics well enough, that they can present creative alternatives for clients.

By being involved at the front end of a project, we can suggest alternative structures and approaches, which might fare better in terms of any review or challenge. Obviously, it is much more difficult to help the client if we are brought in at a later stage. We tell our clients that antitrust considerations are as important as business and financial considerations when planning a deal. If the client incorporates the antitrust considerations into its business analysis, then responses will be readily available to competition questions if the transaction is challenged.

Client Misconceptions

Some clients seem to conceive of antitrust as a set of defined rules, which can be set out in detail and evaluated, like FDA or tax regulations. Unlike those areas of law, there simply are rarely categories, rules or cases in antitrust that can govern specific situations. Rather, antitrust is a mode of analysis, relying heavily on economics. In antitrust law, unlike other areas of the law, you cannot easily or readily rely on prior case law to determine the outcome of your case in your market situation. Past cases simply provide an illustration of the way antitrust law principles were applied to that market situation, to that set of facts. That gives great creative scope for antitrust lawyers, but also creates massive uncertainty for clients.

It helps greatly in simplifying both analysis and recommendations to understand that antitrust is, at its core, simply following the price. That is what I tell all of the clients and junior lawyers. It is the way to analyze the competitive effects of any proposed transaction on claims in litigation. You could have the most restrictive distribution or licensing agreement, or questionable proposed merger imaginable, but if there is no effect on price, it will not have any adverse antitrust consequence.

Recent Major Trends

One of the major changes in antitrust in recent years is the increasing interest in and focus on antitrust issues by other countries, which until now has been virtually nonexistent or widely different. The involvement of the European Commission and some of the national authorities like the German Federal Cartel Office, in antitrust regulation has significantly increased. As a result, today, antitrust lawyers must be aware of the impact of international competition rules and regulators. For an antitrust practice or practitioner not to have a significant transnational component and capability will mean an increasing inability to provide effective assistance.

A second major change is the increasing involvement by state attorneys general in antitrust enforcement. In the last 15 years or so, states have become more involved in antitrust than ever before. Their positions are sometimes congruent with prevailing federal interpretations of antitrust law, but sometimes they are different. The approach to negotiating and litigating, and settling with state attorneys general is different from that with the FTC or DOJ, particularly when actions are brought on a multi-state basis, and antitrust lawyers increasingly must be familiar with the nuances of counseling and litigating in the state enforcement context.

Fairness and Antitrust

Another trend affecting antitrust lawyers is an increasing effort to use state unfair competition laws to challenge business activities. Many complaints now are based more on whether a practice or pricing structure is fair, such as challenges to pharmacy pricing practices or pharmaceutical pricing. It is difficult to deal effectively with challenges from this perspective. To many antitrust practitioners, it seems improper to even have to deal with it because "fairness" is not a concept easily analyzed or dealt with from an economics perspective, as is antitrust law.

There will be struggle in creatively developing modes of economic analysis to assist in responding to unfairness challenges, but it probably can be done. My partners and I have had some success in getting courts to understand that, while a company's business practice may not be one that everybody applauds, it still may be efficient and pro-competitive and that, therefore, it should not be prohibited as unfair competition. The FTC's standards and approach in this area is of help in developing effective responses. If the activity is one which society nonetheless wishes to control, then the proper course is to control that activity by legislation, not by saying that it violates antitrust or unfair competition law. The role that antitrust lawyers can play on this issue is to help develop a competitive analysis, and show that activities that are seemingly unfair or differently applied, may nonetheless be efficient and procompetitive.

Internationalization and Harmonization

Another important trend is the increasing harmonization occurring amongst the international antitrust enforcement agencies. Today, we see cooperation among U.S. agencies and the European Commission and different authorities in the U.K. and Germany that we have not seen in the past. I think everyone has an interest in cooperating. It is certainly frustrating for companies to be faced with conflicting modes of competition analysis and disparate procedures and inconsistent data requests. Companies want a license or distribution arrangement to be assessed similarly in all major jurisdictions. They want an acquisition to be assessed similarly and with similar data. In some respects, it does not matter so much whether the harmonization is the best possible, as long as approaches are harmonized.

We also will see continued pressure for standardization of antitrust rules from both large companies and, increasingly, smaller companies as they become just as international. From the government side, there is the recognition that it does not benefit anyone to simply point fingers and say, "Well, you analyzed it this way because you were favoring your country's manufacturer at the expense of ours." Such harmonization of competition rules is inherently difficult; progress will be slow and fitful. But there is every reason to expect, in view of the economic and political dynamics supporting it, that international harmonization of antitrust standards and approaches will progress.

Consumer Protection and Antitrust

One of the biggest challenges in antitrust remains how to deal with consumer protection issues. Such issues as Internet privacy, telemarketing practices, and direct-to-consumer (DTC) drug advertising have been focuses of enforcement activity by the FTC and the states, and of significant public and political interest. To address consumer protection issues effectively, antitrust lawyers need to become more familiar with, and encourage further development of, information economics. Questions that need to be better addressed include: How do consumers get information? How do they process it? How should they receive it? What are the competitive consequences of providing it? Information economics needs to play a greater role in consumer protection challenges so that advice and decisions can become more analytically sophisticated. Right now, very little economic analysis is part of consumer protection challenges in many instances, and we are left with plaintiffs or consumers who say an activity was unfair, while defendants or sellers say it is fair. That is not a very productive or coherent dialogue to have. A more objective and dispassionate economics-based analysis, that looks at the consequences of information provision in particular contexts, is needed. In consumer protection, as with antitrust analysis a quarter-century ago, we need to develop a framework for economic analysis and a ranking of the importance of the variables involved in the analysis.

The most significant advance in antitrust analysis in the past few decades was the incorporation of sophisticated economic analysis into the decision-making of the antitrust enforcement agencies and the courts. While disputes remain, particularly with respect to analysis of some vertical merger and distribution issues, the general analytical economic framework that has been developed facilitates both analysis and well-accepted, procompetitive conclusions. The extension and development of such an accepted analytical framework in the international and the consumer protection contexts is the challenge for antitrust lawyers for the future.

Stephen Paul Mahinka is a partner in the Washington, D.C. office, manager of the Antitrust Practice, one of the nation's largest, chair of the firm's Life Sciences Interdisciplinary Practice Group, a member of the FDA/Healthcare Regulation Practice, and a member of the firm's Advisory Board. Mr. Mahinka is involved in counseling on and litigation of antitrust and trade regulation matters, and food and drug and healthcare regulation.

Mr. Mahinka's practice includes counseling and litigation concerning mergers and joint ventures; protecting market exclusivity of drug products; product development and FDA approval or clearance of prescription and OTC drugs and dietary supplements; pricing and price discrimination; marketing and advertising; licensing and product promotion and distribution agreements; and Department of Justice (DOJ), Federal Trade Commission (FTC), Food and Drug Administration (FDA) and state investigations.

Mr. Mahinka has published nearly 60 articles on antitrust and FDA/healthcare regulation matters, including FDA and antitrust issues in pharmaceutical industry protection of market exclusivity, energy mergers and joint ventures, multistate antitrust and consumer protection investigations, and pricing, mergers, and vertical relationships in regulated and deregulated industries. He has presented nearly 60 speeches on antitrust and FDA/healthcare regulatory matters at programs sponsored by such groups as the American Bar Association's Section of Antitrust Law and the Food and Drug Law Institute.

Mr. Mahinka served as a law clerk to the Chief Justice of the Massachusetts Appeals Court.

The Qualities of the Successful Antitrust Practitioner

Daniel M. Wall

Chair, Global Antitrust & Competition Practice
Latham & Watkins LLP

The Basics of Antitrust Law

Antitrust law combines the common law approach of case law with economic theory. It reflects an evolving balance between legal and economic concepts, although it is more weighted toward economics today than ever. This is a relatively recent development, having picked up increasing steam over the last 20 years. It has transformed the practice in nearly every respect. Nevertheless, antitrust still also involves traditional common law concepts that every lawyer learns during the first year of law school.

At a practical level, antitrust law is an amalgam of government policy pronouncements, prosecution decisions, judicial decisions and private complaints. There is a whole ecosystem of actors in the antitrust world that are clashing, creating new issues, resolving them and starting the process all over again.

Antitrust laws reflect the philosophy that rivalry among economic actors benefits the consumer and society at large better than government regulation. Because of that, I consider antitrust laws to be anti-regulatory laws. They are based on the belief that if you let people compete independently on their own merits, the consequences will be good enough that we do not need to resort to other, more intrusive kinds of regulation.

There is also a philosophical element to antitrust. The Sherman Act is very much an expression of one of the treasured American philosophies (even if it is by no means unique to Americans), namely that an individual should be able to succeed or fail without the help of others. Antitrust expresses American individualism in an economic setting.

The Antitrust Lawyer

The practice of antitrust law has two basic components: counseling and advocacy. They are quite different skills.

By counseling, I refer to the side of the practice where clients ask for guidance in evaluating the risk of some behavior, in shaping the behavior to minimize risk, and, though this clips into advocacy, in securing approvals for the behavior. This is challenging because the antitrust laws are very general and without interpretation offer almost no useful guidance. I have often said that antitrust law is a concept of applied reasonableness. The trick, therefore, is applying it. Antitrust lawyers interpret the general principles for their clients, turning the generalities into something constructive. We bring antitrust law down to earth.

I believe that counseling is the ultimate test of antitrust expertise. It is very hard to do well. Everything that defines and informs antitrust – the law, economic theory, government policy and business strategy – is in constant motion. And yet to counsel effectively, one must understand both the business and legal/economic sides of the equation. The effective counselor needs to get behind the client's business issues and the business context, such as the structure of their market, and then make a judgment as to how the relatively abstract principles of antitrust law apply. That takes someone who can understand antitrust at a high level. My experience has been that lawyers who just dabble in antitrust miss a lot of important nuances. Counseling in the antitrust area is, in my opinion, for experts only.

Antitrust lawyers are also advocates for our clients. We champion their desires and their causes. Whether they want to do a merger, have been sued, or are the target of an investigation, we articulate in the language of antitrust the reasons they ought to be able to do what they want to do, or perhaps why someone else should not be able to do what they want to do. I find this the most satisfying side of the practice. There is an art to communicating something as subtle and obscure as antitrust theory in an understandable and effective manner. It is quite gratifying when you know you have reached and persuaded your audience.

An antitrust lawyer, like any type of specialized attorney, needs a set of specific skills. First, you need to be able to understand the conduct your client is, or was, involved in. You cannot just know what happened. You have to understand why it happened, why people wanted it to happen and the effects it has had on the market. That requires the acquired skill of knowing how to conduct business analysis and being comfortable with economic concepts. You need to know what drives profit and industry, and what competitive strategy is about. Those are skills which you simply will not have naturally, but rather must be developed over time.

You then need to be able to apply your antitrust learning to the facts, so that you can assess the issues, the outcomes and the probabilities. You need to know a lot about both law and economics to practice in this field. Very few antitrust lawyers can get by predominantly on case law and government pronouncements. The facts change too much, and they are always unique. That's why it's critical to master the principles of economics so that you can apply them to any situation.

An antitrust lawyer also needs advocacy and communication skills. You have to be able to articulate your client's case to a diverse set of audiences. Part of that is based upon innate advocacy and communication skills, but another part is the acquired skill of knowing the most effective ways to explain these things to people. As the years go by, I understand better what will and what will not work in an advocacy situation. Part of this is "dumbing it down," which does not sound like the noblest pursuit. But much more, it is just good teaching. With time you get a sense for what a judge or a jury must first know to understand the important points about your case. I am a firm believer that teaching is the core of good advocacy.

In the antitrust litigation world, there are a lot of people who say they are antitrust lawyers and they are not. They are rather litigators and generalists. Those lawyers tend to be very good at communication, but they do not have the depth of understanding of the business concepts to know what they should be communicating. On the other hand, there are many fabulous antitrust lawyers, particularly those who do a large majority of agency work, who are good analysts, but are not very good communicators. They do not, and should not, litigate.

Different antitrust cases require lawyers with different skill sets. In a price fixing case, where reasonableness is irrelevant and the case is more of a "Who done it?," the client needs a trial lawyer more than an antitrust expert. The client should pick the best trial lawyer possible, and not worry so much about the lawyer's depth of antitrust knowledge. However, that same lawyer would not be appropriate to handle a monopolization case. That lawyer would be overwhelmed by it, because there is such a high level of antitrust analysis in that type litigation. In that case, a great antitrust lawyer is somebody who is an effective trial lawyer and highly skilled at antitrust analysis. If a client is doing a merger review, they will need someone who has a good understanding of merger policy, is a relatively good communicator, and has a lot of experience dealing with the regulatory agencies. So the criteria used when choosing an antitrust lawyer vary depending on what the client needs.

Trying an Antitrust Case

What I find most interesting are antitrust issues that arise when a single firm seeks to implement a strategy that arguably has some exclusionary effects on others. In my opinion, that is the most difficult area of the law and calls for the most sophisticated analysis and advocacy. Throughout the years, I have defended many monopolization cases, which are very challenging. The question is whether an unreasonable restraint on trade occurred. The battle comes down to competing positions over the reasonableness of the conduct. Was there market power? Was it reasonable? Was there a less restrictive alternative? Trying a monopolization case requires the greatest breadth of knowledge and analysis in the antitrust area. Again, the starkest contrast is to price fixing cases, which are essentially disputes over whether it happened or not. If it did, it is illegal. Those cases can be very challenging, but they do not offer the same kind of intellectual challenge as a complicated monopolization case.

To build a case, first you have to understand the client's perspective on the conduct, which means diving into their world. You have to immerse yourself in different industries all the time. For example, right now I am working in the biotech industry, the polyester industry, and the movie distribution industry. They have very little in common. To know an industry from your client's perspective, you have to dig deep. You have to understand what drives the client, what the main components of the competition are, the role of technology, and the role of customer relations. Unless you master all that information, you cannot ever really understand the conduct that you are defending.

Second, you need to understand why this conduct occurred. You can understand that if you have done your homework about the industry. Once you have a good idea of the context and what happened, from experience you start to understand the steps that you have to take to defend the client's actions. Sometimes the defense is rather technical. If you think the case will go to trial, you will need to have witnesses able to articulate your key points. You will bring in economists and work with them so that they will frame the issues in ways that support your arguments.

One of the great challenges in antitrust is the jury trial. You have to deal with jurors who are going to be overwhelmed by the unfamiliarity of the subject matter. In addition, they come in with biases, most of which are bad for the defendant. They will hear the case presented in a limited period of time and in a theatrical style where they do not get to ask the questions that are bugging them. There are such severe limitations on reaching them and educating them that trial can be a bit of a crapshoot. That makes the decision whether to go to trial, risking treble damages, a difficult one.

You will not help your client make that decision by saying that you do not know what will happen at trial. You have to do more than that. I tend to try to do jury research before the trial and I involve the client in that so they can see how jury proxies react to the themes of their case. Often, the client will have a strong-willed CEO who is convinced that a jury will find that what they did was okay. It is sometimes very useful to put that person in front of the mock jury and let them see for themselves that others may not react quite the same way. That process can be quite illuminating. On the other hand, I think it is important not to simply try to talk the client out of doing a trial. Oftentimes, a trial may be the right thing for the client because the settlement demands are just too much or long-term strategic interests are at stake.

Clients vary in the manner in which they make the decision to try or settle. For some, it is a hunch. You discuss the issues with them, and they call it. Others want elaborate analytical methods to help them with these decisions. I will assist the client in making the decision in whatever manner they choose, and I will simply try to put the results into their language.

At trial, the most important thing to do is to simplify, simplify, simplify. The art of taking an antitrust case to trial is figuring out how to simplify the issues while still communicating the equities of your case. When presenting before a jury, you have to come up with simple ways of explaining things and analogies that jurors can relate to from their own experiences. With jury research, we try out different scenes to see if they resonate with lay people or not. If they do, we use them. If not, we discard those approaches and try new ones. We often use graphics to convey simple messages that are capable of being remembered. In the factual picture, we have to try to overcome the fact that perhaps one of the client's people just did something that was sleazy or overbearing. It is critical to anticipate how you are going to deal with that. And, of course, you have to use all of the technical rules of evidence to keep unfavorable evidence out.

In defending an antitrust case you always try two cases at the same time: the technical case and the jury case. That is because it is tough for the defense at trial. The plaintiff's case typically resonates with jurors much more than the defense case. Accordingly, many defense trial victories are actually motions to set aside an adverse jury verdict. That means the defense must put on a technical case that is aimed at the judge and provides the basis for a motion to win as a matter of law at the same time it is trying a more general "fairness" case to the jury. You can't overlook either objective.

A Changing Industry

Near the top of the list of changes in antitrust law is the internationalization of the proceedings. When I started practicing, antitrust law was American law. It seems so quaint today to think of it that way. Today, in my area of specialty – monopolization, you often find yourself in a U.S. and a European investigation. That can occur when adversaries, having failed to convince the U.S. authorities, will complain to the European authorities. Some disputes will arise for the first time overseas. Suddenly the client is much more subject to foreign laws, which are different from ours in material ways. This internationalization of antitrust law has evolved during the last ten years.

Clearly, a long-term trend has been the increasing role of economic analysis in antitrust law. That trend spans my career. I started practicing in 1980, and much of the debate that antitrust law needed to involve more economic analysis took place in the late 1970s, so I witnessed the whole evolution. It has reached a point where today the economic side of the antitrust analysis is in many parts of the law the primary analysis. Merger law is the main example; it is much more driven by economics than by case law. In fact, it is almost pointless to talk about case law in a merger case, because economics is what is truly driving the decision.

For the most part, antitrust laws and cases follow economic developments. High tech became the industry to watch and companies like Microsoft, Intel and biotech companies became the objects of antitrust scrutiny because of their importance to the economy. Meanwhile, the steel companies and the other companies that were targets of many years ago are now struggling and seem like less important objects of inquiry. The natural human tendency is to look to what is currently successful in the economy at large and follow the path there. I have joked that from the standpoint of avoiding government scrutiny, you are better off being involved in a dull industry. On the other hand, I represent a client that is in a joint venture to distribute motion pictures over the Internet. I told them they will always have antitrust issues, because they are simply too interesting.

Technology has affected the practice of antitrust for better and worse. On the plus side, the Internet has greatly changed the way antitrust lawyers gather information for our cases, especially for anything having to do with market power. It is astonishing how much faster we can gather market information. It was hard, in the early '80s, to find good industry information in a hurry. We had to ask for documents and reports. There were lags between when you requested information and when you had any information that you could start to analyze. It is amazing how quickly today that you can get everyone's views, everyone's product information or annual reports.

The other great technological change has been the rise of e-mail. So much of e-mail is essentially a conversation. Now, when people converse, there is a permanent record. The amount of evidence of what people were thinking and what their purposes were is vastly greater than it used to be. It has made the process of crafting or defending against intent arguments quite different than it used to be. Now you can piece together through e-mail the evolution of the activity at issue. That was very evident in the Microsoft case, where they were hurt by their e-mail correspondence. Often people forget the potential future importance of e-mail and create terrible evidence. If they were writing a memo, they would never say these things. It has been an eye-opening experience to see the emergence of e-mail. Unfortunately, when it hurts your client's position, it can be difficult to explain e-mails away at trial, even though a lot of it was flip and not well thought through.

The Future of Antitrust Law

In the future, I do not expect that there will be much standardization of antitrust laws. The goal of harmonization that people have been talking about for ten or fifteen years now is going to remain a goal, not a reality. The differences that exist between nations and continents are rooted in culture and politics and institutions that are not going to change very easily. There will be small steps in the progress of harmonization on the international front. However, the European system is always going to be more intrusive and regulatory because their economic traditions are more intrusive and regulatory. Conversely, in the United States, the words "government regulation" are bad words. In our country, there is a stronger force toward less regulation and more reliance on free trade practices.

In the United States, we have arrived at a very high level of consensus over antitrust policy, certainly higher than I remember in the early part of my career. Back then, there was a fight over incorporating more economics into antitrust law. That issue has died. No one argues over the importance of economic analysis anymore. In fact, there is a certain steadiness now to antitrust law in the United States, and to the extent that there is not, it is because court decisions are much less predictable than policy. At the regulatory level, from the Justice Department and the Federal Trade Commission, rulings are very consistent from one administration to the next. That is a good thing. It certainly does not mean that antitrust law is dead. We still have our debates about particular theories and enforcement programs. But outside those debates, there is still vigorous antitrust enforcement going on. We are bringing more cartel cases than ever, which are non-controversial. In addition, there are many merger challenges. Antitrust agencies are still blocking deals and requesting remedies. However, we do not have the harebrained cases of twenty years ago, where one administration brought a criminal price fixing case against Cuisinart for resale price maintenance. Something like that happening now is inconceivable.

What could be better? I would like to see the whole class action area reformed. Class certification proceedings are all too often a joke, with plaintiffs getting by, and getting classes certified, on intellectually empty arguments that for some reason courts just accept. I have some hope that the recent rule changes allowing for liberalized interlocutory appeals of class certification decisions will help, but it is too early to tell.

In the same part of the antitrust world, I'm ready to support an overhaul of the *Illinois Brick* "indirect purchaser" rule. The Supreme Court's holdings that only the direct purchaser can bring a federal antitrust claim, and in that claim there is no defense that the overcharge was "passed on" downstream, has not turned out to be a great thing for the business community or for the orderly disposition of overcharge cases. Too many states permit indirect purchaser suits under state laws, meaning that we now end up with federal direct purchaser cases and a couple of dozen uncoordinated state indirect purchaser cases. It's an unruly mess. I would federalize the whole thing, prohibiting state indirect purchaser suits under preemption principles, and letting both directs and indirects sue in federal court subject to pass through defenses. That would be more fair and far less costly to deal with.

Daniel M. Wall is a Partner in Latham & Watkins' San Francisco Office and Chair of the Global Antitrust and Competition Practice Group. His practice focuses on complex antitrust litigation, government investigations and counseling, areas in which he has gained national recognition. Mr. Wall's subspecialty is monopolization litigation under Section 2 of the Sherman Act, generally considered the most sophisticated type of antitrust litigation. He has represented in such cases the likes of Intel, Microsoft, Eastman Kodak,

Compaq Computer and Varian Medical Systems. In addition, Mr. Wall has represented clients in dozens of government antitrust investigations spanning the gamut from merger reviews under Hart-Scott-Rodino procedures, to cartel investigations, and to single-firm conduct investigations by the Justice Department, the Federal Trade Commission, and State Attorneys General. Mr. Wall is among the handful of California antitrust lawyers recommended in Chambers USA, Legal Media Group's Expert Guide to Competition and Antitrust Lawyers, and similar publications.

Mr. Wall has been a speaker at numerous continuing legal education and other programs on antitrust, including those sponsored by the ABA Antitrust Section, the Practicing Law Institute, the Conference Board, the National Law Journal Seminars - Press, and National Economic Research Associates. He is a frequent commentator in the media on antitrust issues, including appearances on The NewsHour with Jim Lehrer (PBS), various programming on CNN and CNNfn, CBS Marketwatch, TechTV, and Fox News, and interviews with The New York Times, The Wall Street Journal, Barron's, Business Week, The Los Angeles Times, USA Today and numerous other publications. Mr. Wall is the Founder and Editor-in-Chief of Antitrust Magazine, a publication of the ABA Antitrust Section.

Mr. Wall received his J.D. from the University of Santa Clara in 1980, magna cum laude, and his B.A. from the University of California, Davis.

Advising the Client

Curtis L. Frisbie, Jr.

Partner
Gardere Wynne Sewell LLP

The Basics of Antitrust

Antitrust laws were designed for the ultimate purpose of promoting competition and a free marketplace. Although antitrust laws do not guarantee that all competitors will survive, they do work to prevent the larger, more dominant competitors from taking advantage of their market position in an unfair way to force smaller, less dominant competitors out of business. They also work to insure that consumers pay a market price for their goods and services, and not a price that has been manipulated by the suppliers.

After 30 years of working in the antitrust field, I have noticed several changes in the day-to-day practice, but much of the practice today is the same as it was when I started down this path. Here, I will try to discuss some of the changes and offer some practical tips for various situations that may be encountered.

Representing the Client

Most of my practice involves antitrust litigation. Nevertheless, the role of an antitrust lawyer is not simply to be a trial lawyer. It is to be an advisor. Antitrust lawyers advise their clients on matters having to do with legal versus illegal pricing, distribution of products, trade association activities, cooperation with competitors, and merger and acquisition issues, among others. Basically, the antitrust lawyer's role is to advise the client on what it (and its competitors) can and cannot do safely and legally in the marketplace. Despite there being well over 100 years of settled federal antitrust law, there are still many areas where the law has not yet been well defined. As a result, the most important thing an antitrust lawyer can do for his clients is to determine the relevant legal issues, consider the body of law and then provide an opinion and recommendation based on the possible outcomes. It is simply not enough for an antitrust lawyer to advise his client of the murkiness of the law and that there could be several outcomes, and leave it to the client to choose one of the options. The client deserves an opinion – your best opinion.

Your general goals in representing your client in a litigation situation will vary based on whether your client is the plaintiff or the defendant. If you are a plaintiff's lawyer, your goal should be getting to trial (or a settlement) as quickly as possible. That means getting enough documentary or testamentary evidence to be able to get the case to a jury, without prolonged discovery and pretrial skirmishes. Otherwise, it is too easy to get mired down in trying to create the perfect case, while ultimately not making your client any money on the case, even if you win. If you are a defense lawyer, however, you need to do everything possible to dispose of the case *before* it reaches trial. When a case goes to trial, the skill of the lawyer or the nature of the documents may make little difference in the outcome. If you get a jury that is in the wrong mood on the wrong day, having all the right facts might not make a difference. In any trial, there is the potential for the defendant to lose a great deal of money in actual damages, treble damages, and attorneys' fees, all of which can add up to many millions of dollars. The consequences can be enough to destroy your client's business.

The most interesting situations in antitrust practice come from innovative clients who show an incredible breadth of imagination in what they can do to walk as close to the edge of the cliff of permissible activities without falling over. It is both fun and challenging to deal with a client who has devised a totally new way to sell or distribute a product or make a contract that will allow it some greater advantage over its competitors.

Mergers & Acquisitions Counseling – An Example

I represented a company who had a competitor interested in acquiring it. The company wanted to know whether it was likely that the acquisition would be challenged by the Justice Department. There were only five companies involved in that industry. Unfortunately, the client's company was in an industry in which I had no prior experience, so I did not know how that industry worked. As a result, I asked the company to prepare a great deal of information to inform me about its inner workings and the industry in general. It sent me its 10Ks and 10Qs, annual reports, descriptions of the products it sold, copies of the forms it used to sell the products, and internal documents describing or discussing its competitors. I also asked for information from its trade association, which would explain what the industry looked like, who the other players were, the size of the other players, and their market share and revenues. Once I had that information, I created a list of the types of documents that the government would likely ask for if it were to serve the company with requests for information. I then showed the company how to do an HHI analysis, which is an economic way to analyze a merger by considering what the competitor's market share would likely be prior to and after the acquisition. I then obtained copies of the Department of Justice guidelines for analyzing mergers and HHI numbers. Armed with information about the company's business, the types of products it sold, the companies against whom it competes, and the industry information, I was prepared to sit down with the company and ask whatever questions still needed to be answered. I discussed with the company the standards for evaluating a merger. For each standard, we determined what the company's response would be if the question were asked by the Justice Department. At the end of the process, we were able to conclude that while one particular type of acquisition would present antitrust problems, another type of acquisition would likely not.

The biggest challenge when analyzing a merger or acquisition is determining how the market is going to be defined. Without a precise determination of the relevant product and geographic markets, you cannot shape arguments to the government to justify your transaction. The assistance of an economist can be invaluable, if not absolutely necessary, in most cases to support your conclusions. After all, the government will be using its economists to evaluate the transaction; why go into that battle without a soldier of your own.

Another challenge in merger analysis is that in very complicated industries, where the companies are not selling traditional goods and services, you will need to know the industry backwards and forwards to determine whether or not there are other defenses that might be available. For instance, you should know whether companies in that industry are failing or going out of business at a rapid rate to determine whether the failing company defense, or the failing division and weakened firm defense, may be applicable. You should also know whether a new technology is replacing the industry's present technology since this might suggest a broader product market. You should understand whether there are barriers to entry into that market, such that if the acquisition were to occur, other companies would face a virtually insurmountable hurdle to enter into the market. If that is the case, it will be more likely that the merger will be challenged. If, on the other hand, you can establish that entry into the market is relatively easy and a new entrant could, with the right amount of money and expertise, enter within a short period of time, then the merger will more likely receive approval. Consequently, it is critical when representing a client in a merger or acquisition situation to know the client's industry. If you do not know the client's industry well, then you will not be able to formulate defenses for what might otherwise look to be an indefensible acquisition.

Trying the Case

What if the government announces that if the client were to merge with a competitor, the government will sue? At that point, the company has two options: it can either call off the acquisition or move forward. If it chooses the latter, you would hopefully have done most of your preparation already. At this point, you should have already made an evaluation of the anticompetitive effects of the transaction, met with the Department of Justice at least once, and responded to one or more government requests for documents. It is likely you have already hired an economist/consultant and arranged for him to meet with the Federal Trade Commission or the Justice Department to make your arguments. Essentially, you should have already – in a sense – prepared for trial since you will have told the government what your positions are, learned the positions and arguments of the government, and each of you will have disclosed to the other the factual and economic "evidence" supporting your positions. At this point, you will need to prepare for trial as you would any other civil trial in federal court. You will finish your discovery, develop a trial schedule, get your experts and other witnesses ready, and prepare your opening statements. At that point, deciding the dispute is left up to the judge or jury.

The most eye-opening experience you can have is to take a case to trial, be convinced you should have won, and then have a jury come back with a verdict that is so out of line with anything in reality that it shocks your conscience. I doubt there are many trial lawyers who have not suffered something like that. Most people depend on and believe in the jury system, but the system can go haywire for reasons that do not make much sense. The first thing to do in such a situation is to counsel your client, who is upset to a great degree in part because you previously have told him that you thought you had a great defense in the case and the case was going in well. If you cannot get the judge to set aside the jury verdict, then you have to prepare for a verdict to be entered and start the appeal process. Although this will cost the client more money, it may be the best money spent in the case. For example, in the last 15 years in the Fifth Circuit, less than a handful of antitrust jury verdicts have been upheld. While all circuits do not necessarily have that same defense-oriented record, most antitrust plaintiffs' lawyers recognize that the chances of getting reversed on appeal are fairly high. One well-known and successful plaintiff's lawyer has been quoted as saying he would rather settle all his cases in the future rather than try them and get them appealed.

Counseling Clients & Compliance

In the client's eyes, the antitrust trial process takes too long – normally 2 to 5 years. Unsophisticated clients often do not recognize at the beginning of a case the many costs that are involved, aside from legal fees. For example, there are the costs of document production. The client usually needs to send memos to all of its offices about the lawsuit, instructing its employees not to destroy any applicable documents and to look for the documents that the government or a private plaintiff wants. It is a very laborious process to do document production correctly, and it is expensive in terms of employee time. Indeed, lawyers cannot do it themselves. The process requires direct client participation. There could also be warehousing costs. Sometimes a company will be required to rent an entire warehouse to store documents and hire librarians to keep track of all the documents that are there. There are a lot of hidden costs that a client may not think about ahead of time that can be a source of frustration.

In addition, sometimes clients do not appreciate what might be found during the process. They might uncover documents that they would just as soon not have seen the light of day. There are also the inevitable problems with electronic discovery. Employees write damaging or unhelpful e-mails all the time, and companies do not always appreciate the likelihood that they will be surprised by these e-mail messages, in spite of instructions concerning what not to say and do in e-mail.

I try to respond to client frustrations over cost ahead of time. Once the lawsuit is filed against the client, I sit down with the client and go through the allegations to determine their validity or basis and the defenses. I also work with the client to determine what witnesses we will potentially need to prove certain points. You can determine relatively accurately, within a month or two of receiving the complaint, who is going to have to be deposed on your side, on the other side, the extent of the document production, the warehousing and electronic discovery costs, and what experts will be needed. As the attorney, you should assist your client to plan and budget ahead of time.

Of course, the best way to avoid the costs of litigation is to avoid activities that could lead to litigation in the first place. To that end, I would recommend that most companies initiate an antitrust compliance program. I have been involved in a number of grand jury investigations where employees talk about what they learned in and remember from their antitrust compliance programs. An effective compliance program can have a lasting influence on a client's employees and can save a client many millions of dollars if it keeps the employees from committing antitrust violations. There is no antitrust case that does not cost the company enormous amounts of money. As a result, a company should consider spending a modest amount on antitrust programs to avoid the money pit of litigation further down the road.

Two of the more common antitrust activities include price-fixing and bid rigging. Both can result in enormous civil and criminal penalties.

Companies should therefore stress to their employees to abstain completely from these types of activities, and be serious about it.

Changes and Trends

A continuing change on the criminal side of antitrust law is the use of the Department of Justice's leniency and amnesty policy. The corporate leniency policy was first introduced in 1978 but did not see wide acceptance and use until it was revised in 1993. For instance, the Department of Justice reported in 1999 that it was receiving an average of two leniency applications per month, a rate 20 times higher than under the 1978 program. This revised policy (and the individual leniency policy announced in 1994) has had a profound impact on how antitrust lawyers handle grand jury investigations in criminal cases. Prior to the days of leniency and amnesty, when a company received a grand jury subpoena, it would assume that its industry competitors probably received the same subpoena. The company would then check with its competitors, find out who their lawyers are, and those lawyers would meet and strategize to fight the government together. The lawyers would even let each other know what each other's witnesses testified to during the grand jury hearing and pass that information back and forth pursuant to a joint undertaking privilege. In the past, there was a lot of cooperation amongst the defendants.

Realizing the amount of cooperation existing among defendants, in 1978, the government revamped its policies. It declared that if a company were to discover that it has been involved in an antitrust violation, and if it should tell the government before the government finds out about it on its own, then the government would give the company amnesty. However, in order to receive that amnesty, the company would have to be the first one to "come clean," and cannot have been the ringleader. At that point, the other companies under investigation would become the targets. In order to make the amnesty program more attractive, the policy was revised in 1993 in two significant respects. First, the grant of amnesty was extended to certain situations where the Department of Justice already had an ongoing investigation and, second, amnesty was extended not only to the corporation but also to its officers, directors and employees. That revised policy obviously changed the dynamics between and among defendants very quickly.

Once a grand jury subpoena is served today, the first thing a defense lawyer should do is review the subpoena document requests carefully and quickly go to the company and attempt to determine the Justice Department's potential legal theories (e.g., is their cause of action about bid-rigging or price-fixing or market allocations of some sort?). Usually you would start your investigation with the client's sales department, since that is where most of the activity being investigated would have taken place. You would interview those people expeditiously, find out what they know and locate the potentially relevant documents. A determination must be made quickly whether your client has a major antitrust problem on its hands. Assuming that the investigation uncovers antitrust concerns, at that point, the company must decide whether it wants to wait things out to see if the government indicts them, or whether it should race to meet with the Justice Department in order to seek amnesty. There will almost always be some company willing to be the first in the door in order to receive the advantage of not having their company or employees branded with the criminal indictments; therefore, delay can work against your client.

Additional recent changes in the Department of Justice policy affect the way these quick investigations are being conducted. The new guidelines for the prosecution of business organizations were published January 20, 2003. Sometimes referred to as the "Thompson Memorandum" (named after Larry D. Thompson, Deputy Attorney General in the Department of Justice), the new guidelines attempt to determine the "authenticity" of a company's actual cooperation with a government investigation as part of the process of determining whether to prosecute the business organization. According to the Thompson Memorandum, as a matter of law, a corporation can be held criminally liable for the acts of its directors, officers, employees and agents if the acts were within the scope of corporate duties and intended, at least in part, to benefit the corporation. Therefore, any unsupervised employee committing a crime that benefits the corporation even slightly can potentially expose the corporation to criminal prosecution. While a prosecutor will examine many factors in order to determine the proper treatment of a corporate target, the Thompson Memorandum notes that consideration will be given to the corporation's "willingness to cooperate in the investigation of its agents, including, if necessary, the waiver of corporate attorney-client and work product protection." This waiver would apply to corporate internal investigations and with respect to communications between specific directors, officers and employees and counsel. Some have suggested that the corporation and its counsel are being deputized to assist the government prosecute the case.

The impact of the Thompson Memorandum is that it now may be more difficult for corporate counsel to take a quick look and gather the facts necessary to determine whether the corporation is facing antitrust liability so that amnesty or immunity can be considered. Employees may not want to talk to corporate counsel without having counsel of their own. Employees may view the corporation and corporate counsel as the enemy, who has been enlisted by the government to aid the government and not the employee.

A collateral problem also arises in the context of civil suits. If a corporation acquiesces to the government demand for a waiver of the attorney-client or work product privileges, it has arguably destroyed the privileges for discovery in the antitrust civil suits that certainly will follow. Indeed, amnesty from criminal prosecution does not protect a company from the private civil suits relating to the same activity. Although the government is sworn to secrecy with regard to grand jury activities, the fact of the investigation usually leaks out. And once that information is publicized, plaintiff's lawyers begin searching for a client to serve as a plaintiff, such as a purchaser of those goods or services. There often will be several suits filed all over the country. Lawyers in charge of the various suits then engage in side-litigation to determine where all the federal suits should be consolidated. Thus, seeking amnesty might free your client from criminal prosecution, but it could set off a powder keg of explosive civil litigation. Yet in the same vein, legislation is being considered that would place a cap on civil damages in cases where the wrongdoer has earned amnesty from criminal punishment.

Another recent trend in the antitrust field is the proliferation of state antitrust cases. While state antitrust laws have existed for decades – in fact, the antitrust laws of Kansas pre-date the 1890 Sherman Act – as a practical matter, antitrust cases were generally filed in the federal courts. That has now changed. More antitrust cases are now being filed in the state courts because of the perception that federal cases take too long to reach a disposition. On the other hand, state cases – where dockets are less crowded – are believed to reach trial much quicker. Another reason to file state cases is to avoid consolidation with multiple other cases, as is common in the federal system.

Another trend is the increasing number of Attorney General Cases, where 10 or 15 states will cooperate to bring a single action against a company or group of companies that they perceive to be engaging in illegal antitrust activity. Based on a variety of reasons, more class action lawsuits, antitrust and RICO cases are also being filed today than had been in the past. All over the United States, legislative bodies are passing increasingly stringent tort reform laws. These laws have reduced or eliminated the amount of punitive damages that can be awarded, shortened statutes of limitations, and capped the economic damages on medical malpractice claims. Over time, these reforms have severely cut into the practices of plaintiffs' personal injury lawyers. As a result, these lawyers have begun to seek out cases where they could make as much money as before, notwithstanding the tort reforms. One solution has been to bring class action lawsuits and lawsuits involving claims that allow treble damages. Therefore, class action lawsuits and antitrust and RICO cases are now being filed more often by lawyers who traditionally have not operated in those spheres.

Globalization is yet another change in the antitrust field. More cases are now being brought that allege price-fixing activities outside of the United States, but with an impact on the United States economy. It is clear that in the future, we are going to have many more cases with an international flair to them.

Final Advice

There are two types of an antitrust practice: civil practice and a criminal practice with a government agency as the opponent. When dealing with government agencies, the most important tip I can offer is to be absolutely candid with them. Tell them the answers to their questions or tell them that for whatever reason, you cannot answer their questions. It is critical to maintain the trust and confidence of agency officials beyond the current situation because you will have to deal with those same people on numerous other occasions for the same or different clients over the course of many years. The private antitrust cases brought on the civil side vastly outnumber the government cases. With regard to those cases,

I have always tried to maintain basically the same policy of candor. As a result, I have had very few problems with opposing lawyers, which has given my clients a distinct advantage in litigation.

A well-known trial lawyer, Curt Frisbie has more than 30 years of trial experience. He handles major antitrust and other commercial litigation matters such as securities fraud, shareholder derivative actions, and patent, trademark and copyright cases. He has substantial experience defending class action cases. Mr. Frisbie also advises businesses on pricing plans, distributor agreements and antitrust corporate compliance programs.

Mr. Frisbie has represented, among many others Brook Mays Music Company, Flowers Industries, Inc., The AIG Companies, Southwestern Bell Telephone Co., and Tyler Pipe Industries, Inc. Mr. Frisbie has participated in the trial of 13 antitrust cases, as well as other business litigation and class action disputes.

Mr. Frisbie is admitted to practice before the United States Supreme Court, United States Court of Appeals for the 5th, 8th, 10th and 11th Circuits, the United States District Courts of Texas, Northern District of Georgia, and Eastern District of Wisconsin, and the Texas Supreme Court. He received his J.D. from St. Mary's University School of Law in 1971 and his B.S. from the University of Alabama in 1966.

Preserve, Protect and Defend:

Dealing Fairly and Squarely with Clients in Antitrust Law Practice

Keith E. Rounsaville

Stockholder and Chair of Antitrust Practice
Akerman Senterfitt

A Brief Overview of Antitrust Statutes.[1]

The Sherman Act

The purpose of antitrust law is to eliminate and prevent artificial restraints on output of goods and services, because those restraints result in lower-quality goods and services and higher prices to consumers. The Sherman Act is the most important antitrust statute. For a statute of such importance, its key provisions have relatively few words. Judicial interpretations of them would fill many library shelves, as would the scholarly commentary and criticism which they have generated.

Section One of the Sherman Act[2] prohibits "every contract, combination or conspiracy" in restraint of trade; that is, concerted activity of two or more entities to reduce output or increase prices. The Supreme Court long ago determined that concerted activity by participants at the same level of the distribution chain – "horizontal restraints" – are more likely to harm competition than concerted activity by participants at different levels of the distribution chain – "vertical restraints." The Court devised legal standards which condemn many horizontal restraints as conclusively anticompetitive or "illegal *per se*." Many *per se* illegal horizontal restraints, including price-fixing, bid-rigging, and geographic market allocation, are prosecuted as felonies by the U.S. Department of Justice. Only one vertical restraint, minimum resale price-fixing, is treated as *per se* illegal.

Other vertical restraints are evaluated under the "rule of reason," which requires an examination of the effect of the restraint on competition in a relevant market. Vertical restraints, including minimum resale price maintenance, are not subjects of criminal prosecution.

---

[1] I omit the Clayton Act in this discussion, because §3 has effectively been subsumed by §1 of the Sherman Act, and §7, which governs certain mergers and acquisitions, is not a statute which I apply frequently in my practice.
[2] 15 U.S.C. §1 (2000).

Section Two of the Sherman Act[3] addresses anticompetitive exercises of market power by single firms,[4] which by themselves can reduce their output and increase prices without losing significant sales to competitors. Such firms often do business in markets in which barriers to entry, such as patents or regulation, inhibit new entry into the market. Merely being a monopolist does not violate Section Two. Rather, to violate Section Two, a firm which has monopoly power must engage in anticompetitive conduct which excludes or eliminates one or more competitors.

A goal of antitrust laws is to preserve freely competitive markets for goods and services. A freely competitive market is one in which the output of goods and services will match the demand for them at prices that equal their marginal cost. This price level includes some level of profit for efficient producers. Of course, all producers are not equally efficient, and less efficient producers often fail in a functioning competitive market. The Sherman Act was not intended to prevent inefficient competitors from failing. Contrary to expectations of failed businesspersons, the antitrust laws do not create or preserve a "level playing field."

The Robinson-Patman Act

The Robinson-Patman Act[5] ("RPA") is an important exception to the general proposition that the purpose of antitrust laws is to prevent and eliminate unreasonable restraints on output and prices. The RPA was enacted in the 1930's as a measure to preserve "mom and pop" grocery stores by curbing the buying power of the rapidly expanding retail grocery chains. The primary objective of the RPA was to limit "price

---

[3] 15 U.S.C. § 2 (2000).

[4] Section Two also contains a conspiracy offense, which has been treated similarly as violations of Section One.

[5] The RPA amended § 2 of the Clayton Act of 1936, 15 U.S.C. §§ 13-13b, 21a (2000).

discrimination,"[6] which enabled retail grocery chains to purchase large quantities of products more cheaply than the "mom and pops" could purchase them and to resell those products at prices lower than "mom and pops" could profitably resell the same products. Price discrimination is simply the sale of the same product to different customers at different prices. For many years, the RPA has been criticized by economists and antitrust scholars, because it inhibits price competition by requiring sellers to sell their products to competing purchasers at the same prices.

The RPA does not prohibit all price discrimination in sales to competing customers. The RPA permits a seller to demonstrate that a lower price to a customer is "cost-justified" or that it "meets" the lower price offered by a competing seller to a favored customer. In litigation, seeking to hold a seller liable for price discrimination, the RPA has the "virtue" of having several elements which the plaintiff must prove to establish liability.

The Revolution in Antitrust Litigation in the Last Quarter of the Twentieth Century

The RPA is the major anomaly of antitrust law which survived the revolution in antitrust law following the Supreme Court's 1977 decision in *Continental T.V., Inc. v. GTE Sylvania, Inc.* ("*Sylvania*").[7] The purpose of antitrust law and the relationship between antitrust law and economics were often unclear during the first 75 years after the Sherman Act was enacted. A revolution in the application of antitrust law in litigation was set in motion by *Sylvania*, and that revolution eliminated apparently

---

[6] Other provisions of the RPA prohibit fictitious brokerage (§ 2(c)), requiring sellers to grant advertising and promotional allowances to competing customers on proportionately equal terms. §§ 2(d), 2(e)

[7] 433 U.S. 36 (1977).

conflicting goals of antitrust enforcement and firmly established the economic foundation of antitrust law.

Sylvania provided the foundation for two progressive developments in the enforcement of antitrust law. First, the Supreme Court embraced the "rule of reason" as the presumptive standard to be applied in litigation to evaluate most concerted restraints of trade. Specifically, the Court adopted the rule of reason as the standard which must be applied to vertical non-price restraints, and the Court made the rule of reason the presumptive standard to be applied to any restraint with which courts lacked sufficient experience to predict that it always, or nearly always, injured competition. Second, the Court adopted an economic interpretation of antitrust law, espoused by the "Chicago School," which forced federal judges to examine economic effects of various restraints and to evaluate possible procompetitive justifications for them.

In 1979, the Supreme Court reinforced these two aspects of *Sylvania* in *Broadcast Music, Inc. v. CBS*,[8] in which the Court declined to apply the *per se* rule to an efficiency-enhancing price-fixing arrangement. In 1984, in *NCAA v. Board of Regents*[9], the Court declined to apply the *per se* rule to an association of universities which limited the number of college football games which could be broadcast on television and found that the rule of reason should be applied to a facially horizontal restraint on output. The restraint did not withstand analysis under the rule of reason, but the Court again communicated to lower courts that, except for a few "hard core" restraints, most antitrust cases required examination of economic consequences of restraints in the context of a relevant market.

---

[8] 441 U.S. 1 (1979)
[9] 486 U.S. 85 (1984)

The next important developments in the revolution in antitrust litigation occurred in 1986. Those developments were partly procedural and partly substantive. The procedural development is embodied in three cases, known as the "trilogy": *Anderson v. Liberty Lobby*,[10] *Celotex Corp. v. Catrett*[11] and *Matsushita Industrial Elec. Co. v. Zenith Radio Corp.*,[12] in which the Supreme Court clarified the evidentiary standards and methodology for lower federal courts to apply in ruling on motions for summary judgment. The procedural effect of the trilogy was that it facilitated summary disposition in factually baseless antitrust cases before trial. Most lower courts enthusiastically embraced the trilogy. Almost overnight, private antitrust cases changed from being among the most difficult in which to obtain summary disposition to among the easiest, on two distinct grounds: failure to prove the existence of conspiracy, which is an essential element in all § 1 Sherman Act cases; and failure to prove the relevant market and the market power of the defendant in the relevant market, which are requirements in § 1 rule of reason cases and § 2 monopolization and attempt to monopolize cases.

The development in substantive antitrust law was contained in *Matsushita*, in which the Court emphasized that ambiguous, circumstantial evidence is insufficient as a matter of law to support an inference of conspiracy. Instead, to survive a motion for summary judgment, a plaintiff must present evidence "which tends to exclude the possibility that the alleged conspirator acted independently."[13]

Experienced litigators who defend antitrust cases now focus their discovery efforts on laying a foundation for demonstrating the absence of a genuine issue of material fact concerning one or more elements of the

---

[10] 475 U.S. 574 (1986)
[11] 477 U.S. 242 (1986)
[12] 477 U.S. 317 (1986)
[13] 475 U.S. at 588

plaintiff's claim and routinely move for summary judgment at the conclusion of discovery.

In 1993, the Supreme Court decided *Daubert v. Merrill Dow Pharmaceuticals, Inc.,*[14] which initiated the final major development in the revolution in antitrust litigation. *Daubert* was not an antitrust case. Its importance in antitrust litigation arises from the requirement that issues such as definition of the relevant product market and proof of market power be based on expert testimony. In *Daubert*, the Court articulated several standards for trial courts to apply in evaluating and excluding unreliable expert testimony. *Daubert* dealt specifically with "scientific" evidence. The Court confirmed that the *Daubert* principles apply to all expert testimony in *Kumho Tire Co. v. Carmichael.*[15]

Daubert had an immediate impact on antitrust litigation. Nobel laureates in economics can no longer offer opinions concerning economic issues in an antitrust case simply because they are Nobel laureates in economics. If the proposed expert opinion testimony does not pass muster under the tests for reliability described in *Daubert* and *Kumho* (which have been incorporated into Rule 702 of the Federal Rules of Evidence), it will be found to be inadmissible before trial, and may result in summary judgment against the proponent of the testimony. Pretrial motions to exclude expert testimony under *Daubert* are now routine in antitrust litigation.

With the adoption in 2000 of amended Rule 702 of the Federal Rules of Evidence, the Twentieth Century ended with antitrust law and antitrust litigation practice which were vastly different from those when the Court decided *Sylvania* in 1977.

---

[14] 509 U.S. 579 (1993)
[15] 526 U.S. 137 (1999)

Where Antitrust Issues May Arise

In my practice, I have represented many corporations which have been the targets of federal grand jury investigations of "hard core" antitrust violations (bid-rigging, price-fixing, or market allocation schemes). The industries in which I have represented clients who were indicted for or charged by information with criminal antitrust violations shared the following characteristics:

They involved products which were fungible and were not differentiated by advertising or brand loyalty; for example, asphalt road paving, rebar steel, chain-link fence, school milk and metal building insulation.

Demand for the product was declining and excess production capacity existed.

A relatively few competitors in a region controlled most sales.
The competitors had frequent opportunities to meet, often at trade shows and industry conventions.
Individuals with control over regional pricing decisions believed that stable market shares could be achieved by reducing production and raising price levels, and that they could detect and punish "cheating."

Fortunately, I have represented many clients who participated in industries which shared many of the foregoing characteristics and who were not charged with criminal antitrust violations. In those cases, the coordinated activity that prosecutors observed was simply "oligopoly pricing" by a few competitors who had access to excellent, readily available market intelligence and who understood how their competitors perceived and responded to their pricing decisions. I have also represented many clients in private antitrust lawsuits in which plaintiffs claimed to be injured by parallel behavior of participants in oligopoly markets.

For years, I have represented clients who bought or sold products in industries in which participants were ignorant of, or, in any event, ignored the RPA. For example, sellers of products in many industries offer discounts which are based entirely on quantity purchased, with price breaks set at arbitrary levels; for example, x% off for 50,000 units; y% off for 250,000 units. The sellers make no effort to determine whether these price differentials are justified by costs savings and explain that "everyone in the industry does it this way." Unfortunately for them, the RPA does not recognize an "everyone does it" defense.

Experience has taught me that antitrust violations can be deterred, or at least detected early, if a corporate employer is committed to educating its employees about complying with antitrust laws. In today's business environment, hard core antitrust violations rarely result from ignorance of the law. Most business executives know, for example, that they cannot agree with their competitors on the prices or price levels at which they will sell their products.

In my experience, price-fixing schemes were concocted by rogue employees, who knew that their actions were illegal and also violated written policies of their employers. In such cases, a co-worker who was trained in antitrust compliance and who understood his responsibility to report suspicious conduct to a designated compliance officer could have saved his employer millions of dollars in fines, damages and attorney's fees. The financial consequences of not adopting and implementing an antitrust compliance program far exceed the cost of conducting regular seminars in antitrust compliance for executives, managers and employees who are involved in pricing, credit and production decisions and in sales.

Protocol for Investigating a Suspected Criminal Antitrust Violation. Advice and Considerations Preceding an Investigation. Discovery of the Problem and Initial Advice to the Client.

During the thirty plus years that I have practiced in the area of antitrust litigation, counseling and compliance, I have been successful in assisting clients "nip in the bud" potential antitrust disasters. Even when the bud was not nipped early enough to avoid all adverse consequences, I was able to negotiate a satisfactory, and less expensive, resolution of criminal antitrust problems with antitrust enforcement authorities. I have achieved these results by conducting a *private* investigation of my client.

Attorneys often learn by accident that a client has a potentially serious antitrust problem. For example, while performing legal services for a corporate client in a routine engagement, an attorney may discover documents or other factual information which indicates that the client is participating in concerted activity with competitors that can be prosecuted as a criminal violation[16] of Section 1 of the Sherman Act. Or, an employee of the client may request advice from an attorney about activity which he/she suspects may be illegal under the antitrust laws.[17]

Confronted with such information, the attorney must not ignore it. Of course, the attorney cannot require the client to take action to address the problem.[18] Nevertheless, the attorney must provide the client

---

[16] In recent years, criminal prosecutions under the Sherman Act have been limited to "hard core" conduct among competitors, including bid-rigging, horizontal price-fixing, horizontal market allocation and horizontal customer allocation.

[17] This discussion assumes that neither the client nor the attorney has information that a law enforcement agency is investigating the suspicious conduct.

[18] If the client refuses to follow the attorney's advice concerning appropriate steps to respond to a potentially serious problem that could adversely affect the

unambiguous notice of the seriousness of the problem and make preliminary recommendations about how the client should deal with it. At a minimum, the attorney should orally: [19]

Explain to the client the potential direct and collateral consequences of participating in conduct which constitutes a criminal violation.

Recommend that the client act immediately to terminate the client's participation in the conspiracy and withdraw from the conspiracy, and investigate the nature and extent of the client's participation in the conspiracy.

Requirements for Withdrawal from a Conspiracy

Termination of participation in a conspiracy does not extinguish a participant's liability for the continuing acts of coconspirators or for the continuing effects of the conspiracy. A conspirator may avoid further liability for acts and effects of the conspiracy only by withdrawing from it.

Withdrawal from an antitrust conspiracy requires more than cessation of the activity. [20] After having entered a conspiracy, a conspirator is presumed, as a matter of law, to remain a member of the conspiracy unless and until it undertakes "affirmative steps, inconsistent with objects of the conspiracy, to disavow or to defeat the conspiratorial objectives." [21]

---

value or viability of the client, the attorney may wish to terminate the representation.

[19] The attorney must carefully document the file regarding providing this advice.

[20] *Morton's Market, Inc. v. Gustafson's Dairy, Inc.*, 198 F.3d 823, 838 (11th Cir. 1999).

[21] *Id.*

A comprehensive investigation of the nature and extent of the client's participation is essential to enable counsel to assess the client's exposure in criminal and civil proceedings and to make recommendations to the client about actions that must be taken to respond to the findings and conclusions of the investigation. Such an investigation will enable counsel to evaluate whether making a disclosure to law enforcement authorities will be the only effective option to accomplish withdrawal. And the investigation may enable counsel to advise the client whether notifying other coconspirators of the client's withdrawal will expose the client to economic retaliation by coconspirators or whether notice will trigger a race to report the conspiracy to law enforcement authorities.

Self-Reporting and Leniency

The Antitrust Division of the U.S. Department of Justice contends that reporting a price-fixing conspiracy to a law enforcement agency — preferably the Antitrust Division — is the only effective way to "disavow or defeat the objectives of the conspiracy." The Antitrust Division has adopted a corporate leniency program specifically designed to encourage members of criminal antitrust conspiracies to report the illegal activity and to cooperate with any resulting investigation and prosecutions of other participants. The benefit of self-reporting and cooperation is immunity from criminal prosecution for the corporation and cooperating employees. Immunity from criminal prosecution does not extend to liability in civil treble damages lawsuits by private plaintiffs.

Before an attorney can competently advise a client to self-report, the attorney must have complete knowledge of the conduct of the client to be reported. An attorney who approaches prosecutors to disclose a client's wrongdoing without fully understanding the extent and implications of the client's wrongdoing creates huge risks for the client and for the attorney as the inevitable investigation unfolds. Thus, the attorney cannot safely accept the client's version of relevant facts. Only a comprehensive independent investigation will suffice to ascertain the facts.

Five Stages of a Comprehensive Investigation

A comprehensive investigation of potential violations of antitrust laws of the United States (and other countries) should proceed in five stages. Except for the Fifth Stage, Education and Compliance, each stage is an essential precondition to the next stage.

First Stage: Authorization and Directive from the Board of Directors
To demonstrate that the Company (1) has terminated its participation in the conspiracy, (2) is undertaking affirmative steps to defeat or disavow the purpose of the conspiracy and (3) is seriously committed to conducting a thorough investigation of potential antitrust violations, Board action is required to authorize the investigation and to require officers and employees to cooperate with the investigation.
Preferably, at one Board meeting, the following actions should be taken, with counsel present to preserve confidentiality:

Counsel should advise the Board that potential antitrust problems involving the Company appear to have occurred and that various resolutions from the Board of Directors are necessary to respond to those problems.

Counsel should advise the Board of the nature of the conduct that is known or suspected but should avoid disclosing incriminating details. As importantly, counsel must advise the Board of the potential direct and collateral consequences of the Company's participation in criminal antitrust activity.

The Board must adopt a resolution which condemns, repudiates and disavows any illegal activities or arrangements involving the Company and its employees and which directs that all such activities or arrangements cease immediately.

Assuming that counsel has been employed, the Board should adopt a resolution instructing counsel to conduct a thorough investigation of any potential antitrust violations, to report to the Board the results of the investigation and to make appropriate recommendations to respond to any problems which are uncovered.

The Board must direct all officers and employees of the Company to cooperate fully with the investigation.

Second Stage: Collecting and Reviewing Documents
Outside counsel will provide a list of categories of documents for which responsible employees of the Company must make a thorough search of all files in which documents responsive to any listed category are likely to be contained.

Outside counsel must have access to all documents, including documents stored on electronic media, such as electronic mail, which may indicate the existence and extent of potential violations of the antitrust laws.

Under the direction of a senior officer of the Company and outside counsel, documents will be collected and sent to one or more locations for review. If responsive documents are located outside the United States, they probably should not be sent to the United States for review.

The collected documents will be reviewed thoroughly by outside counsel, who will determine whether additional documents must be gathered.

Third Stage: Interview of Persons Who May Have Knowledge or Information about Potential Violations of Antitrust Laws

After review of documents has been completed, outside counsel will conduct interviews of each person who they believe has or may have knowledge of information relevant to the potential violations of the antitrust laws.[22]

The identity of the persons to be interviewed will be determined initially from the review of documents and from persons known from other sources to have knowledge of information relevant to potential antitrust violations.

When employee(s) provide information which counsel reasonably believes may lead to a disclosure that the employee(s) participated in criminal conduct, outside counsel must advise the employee(s) to consult his/her own attorney before proceeding with the interview.

The interview(s) of employee(s) suspected of participating in illegal conduct should not proceed without the express approval or outside the presence of the employee(s)' personal counsel.

As interviews proceed, other persons who may have relevant knowledge may be identified, and they, too, will be interviewed.

If some or all employees are foreign nationals who do not reside in the United States, careful thought must be given to the location of their interviews. For several reasons, interviews of foreign nationals who do not reside in the United States should probably not be conducted in the United States.

---

[22] Preliminary interviews may be appropriate before documents are collected to determine what documents may exist and where relevant documents are located. Frequently, knowledgeable employees will be interviewed several times during an investigation.

The interviews will continue until outside counsel is satisfied that the extent of potential violations has been fully explored.

Fourth Stage: Preparation of Report and Report to Directors
Upon completion of interviews, outside counsel will prepare a report of findings and conclusions for the Board of Directors.

Outside counsel will more than likely make an oral report[23] to the Board of the scope of any illegal conduct that was discovered. Counsel will again explain to the Board the direct and collateral consequences to the Company of its participation in the suspected illegal activity.

Outside counsel will make recommendations to the Board for actions to assure that any problems which were discovered are addressed appropriately.

Recommendations will likely include matters such as terminating or suspending employees suspected of being involved in the illegal conduct, making restitution to victims of the conspiracy and taking other actions which disavow or defeat the purpose of the conspiracy.

Especially if involved employees are to be suspended or terminated, counsel will describe to the Board, the Company's risks and benefits of making application for leniency to appropriate law enforcement agencies and, if the application is accepted, making full disclosure of illegal activities to those agencies.

Simultaneous applications for leniency in several jurisdictions may be necessary. Law enforcement authorities in several foreign jurisdictions,

---

[23] Counsel will likely retain any written report and work product from the investigation in counsel's files.

including those in Canada, the United Kingdom and the European Union, have adopted leniency programs which are modeled on the DOJ's leniency program.

If the Company does not already have a written antitrust compliance policy and an antitrust compliance program, outside counsel will present to the Board of Directors a written antitrust compliance policy and a written antitrust compliance program, which should be adopted by the Board, with directions to appropriate officers for prompt implementation.

Fifth Stage: Education and Compliance

If the Company does not already have an antitrust compliance program, such a program must be adopted and implemented promptly.[24]

Antitrust compliance training is an important aspect of the Company's affirmative action to "disavow the purpose" of the antitrust conspiracy and thereby to withdraw from it.

Whether the Company has an existing antitrust compliance program or has just adopted one, the Company must implement the policy and program by conducting seminars and taking other appropriate steps to emphasize to all officers and employees whose job functions involve certain activities, such as pricing of products, sales, production, credit and transportation, concerning their own and the Company's responsibilities to comply with the antitrust laws of all countries in which the Company is doing business.

Seminars and other antitrust compliance training should be conducted at least annually.

---

[24] The Company need not await the results of the investigation to adopt and implement an antitrust compliance policy and program.

In addition to providing for compliance training, the antitrust compliance program must contain (a) procedures for employees to report suspected antitrust violations anonymously and without fear of retaliation; (b) procedures to investigate such reports; and (c) disciplinary actions, including termination and nonpayment of attorney's fees, to be taken when an employee is found to have violated the Company's antitrust compliance policy.

Challenges in Counseling Clients

Keeping the client informed of developments in a case is crucial to the client and to the attorney. I send to the client copies of nearly every piece of correspondence and every paper filed with the court. Clients do not like to be surprised by bad news about a lawsuit. If I see a problem early in a case, I explain to my client how it may play out, if I am not certain; and how it will play out, if I know. For example, I have represented clients in criminal antitrust investigations in which senior management professed absolute confidence that there was not a problem. During interviews of employees, I learned that at least one employee, and possibly more, had serious exposure to indictment. Or, I received a telephone call from an attorney who represented another subject of the investigation and was advised that he must withdraw from our joint defense group. The unspoken message was clear: his client had made a deal with the prosecutor to testify against coconspirators, at least one of whom was employed by my client.

I did not keep this bad news to myself. I immediately requested a meeting with appropriate representatives of the client and advised them that I knew what we should do, and why we should do it. When the information caused me to conclude that (a) indictment of an employee or the client was imminent, and/or (b) a senior level executive had participated in criminal activity, I requested a meeting with the Board of Directors.

During a criminal investigation, I meet regularly with "need to know" executives to give them progress reports. My reports are not inevitably pessimistic, and I am careful not to reveal more information than they should know. But when an adverse development has occurred, or when I foresee that an adverse development will likely occur, I inform the people who have need to know that information.

A major problem in many huge cases that have received much publicity recently is that lawyers failed to remember that their client was the corporation, not the executives, who often participated in creating the problem. When senior executives *are* the problem, the lawyer must bypass them and report directly to the Board. Obtaining access to the Board can be very difficult, but the Board has the responsibility of dealing with the problem, including terminating or suspending senior executives.

Keeping open lines of communication with the client is the best way that I know to avoid problems with the client. In a highly publicized case, a lawyer faces the added burden of attempting to manage information released by the public relations department. The "tell 'em nothing, and tell 'em slow" attitude toward information management can be disastrous in today's environment. Many people, and particularly media representatives, interpret "no comment" as an admission of guilt. A "no comment" response to a newspaper reporter can be more devastating to a corporation's credibility, sales and stock price than a statement of sympathy for victims or a qualified acceptance of responsibility.

Depending on the circumstances of a particular case, it may be necessary to have a corporate officer serve as a spokesperson for the corporation in order to provide a "human face" to the public. Selecting the right spokesperson can be perilous for the company and for the individual selected. The individual who makes public announcements or press releases should be someone who is not exposed to prosecution or to civil liability. Any public statement must be verifiably true. Public announcements must be drafted so that they are neither overly optimistic nor overly pessimistic to minimize their effect on the stock price.

Information management during a crisis has become a specialty for some lawyers who practice in the antitrust arena. Lawyers frequently disagree about public relations strategies. Adverse consequences of bad publicity sometimes cannot be avoided, but they sometimes can be alleviated by maintaining open lines of communication with the client and by keeping the client informed.

A Trend toward Filing Antitrust Claims and Tort Claims for Anticompetitive Conduct in State Court

Many attorneys accustomed to defending antitrust cases in federal court have observed that state enforcement authorities and attorneys for private plaintiffs have more frequently been filing complaints in state courts. In some respects, this trend reflects more favorable state substantive antitrust law and procedural and evidentiary advantages in state court. It also reflects recognition by plaintiff's attorneys that proving most antitrust claims in federal court requires expert testimony to establish market power and that many, if not most, private antitrust cases in federal court end with summary judgment for the defendant.

Plaintiff's attorneys are frequently electing to avoid filing claims altogether, preferring to assert claims for various common law and statutory torts in state court, where the prospect of reaching a jury is much higher than in federal court, and a reasonable possibility exists for an award of punitive damages which are equal to or greater than treble damages.

Price-Fixing Claims against Indirect Purchasers

In *Illinois Brick Co. v. Illinois*,[25] the Supreme Court, as a matter of pragmatic judicial policy, held that, except in narrowly defined circumstances, only direct purchasers can sue for overcharges resulting from a conspiracy to fix prices in violation of § 1 of the Sherman Act. Shortly after *Illinois Brick* was decided, several states passed so-called "*Illinois Brick* repealers," which expressly permit indirect purchaser suits under state antitrust laws. In *California v. ARC America Corp.*,[26] the Supreme Court held that those state laws are valid and enforceable. Now, twenty states and the District of Columbia have antitrust statutes which expressly permit indirect purchasers to sue for price-fixing violations.

Courts in other states have held that indirect purchasers can recover price-fixing overcharges under state deceptive and unfair trade practices acts. Typically, these statutes provide causes of action for consumers against persons or firms who engage in "unfair methods of competition" or "unfair and deceptive acts or practices," as those terms are interpreted by the Federal Trade Commission or by federal courts under § 5(a)(1) of the Federal Trade Commission Act. For example, a Florida appellate court held that indirect purchasers who have been damaged by illegal

---

[25] 431 U.S. 720 (1977)
[26] 490 U.S. 93 (1989)

price-fixing have standing[27] to bring actions under the Florida Deceptive and Unfair Trade Practices Act.[28]

Plaintiffs asserting indirect purchaser claims may prefer to file suit in state court, for a variety of reasons, including more favorable summary judgment standards under state law than under federal law since the Supreme Court's "trilogy."

Lawsuits in State Court Under State Antitrust Laws

Some state antitrust statutes are considered by plaintiff's attorneys to provide more favorable theories for recovery than are available under federal antitrust statutes. Other state antitrust statutes are directly modeled after federal statutes[29] and are intended to be interpreted consistently with federal court interpretations of those statutes.[30] State antitrust statutes typically eliminate the federal requirement that the activity or conduct affect interstate or foreign commerce.[31]

Many plaintiff's attorneys believe that their state law antitrust claims have a better chance of being decided by a jury in state court than in federal court. Even antitrust claims based on conduct such as horizontal price-fixing, which is illegal *per se* under federal antitrust law and under most state antitrust laws, require proof of an illegal agreement or conspiracy. A plaintiff's conspiracy evidence which would not be sufficient to survive a motion for summary judgment under the standards

---

[27] *Mack v. Bristol-Meyers Squibb Co.*, 673 So.2d 100 (Fla. 1st DCA 1996)

[28] Section 501.201, *et seq.,* Fla. Stat.

[29] *See, e.g.,* §§ 542.18 and 542.19, Fla. Stat.

[30] *See, e.g.,* § 542.32, Fla. Stat.

[31] *See, e.g.,* § 542.31, Fla. Stat.

articulated by the Supreme Court in the "trilogy"[32] may, nevertheless, be sufficient under less stringent summary judgment standards established by state supreme courts.

Moreover, most antitrust violations require proof of a relevant market and sufficient power in the relevant market to affect prices. In antitrust cases in federal court, the relevant market and market power must be established by expert testimony, which meets the tests of reliability announced in *Daubert v. Merrill Dow Pharmaceuticals, Inc.*,[33] now embodied in Rule 702 of the Federal Rules of Evidence. Many state courts, including those in Florida, apply less rigorous standards for admissibility of expert testimony than are applied in federal court.

Lawsuits in State Courts Asserting Common Law Tort Claims

For many years, plaintiff's attorneys were attracted to filing private actions for violations of federal antitrust laws by the automatic trebling of damages and recovery of attorney's fees which are awarded to successful plaintiffs.[34] These remedies are often available in state antitrust statutes.[35]

The lure of treble damages and attorney's fees are not enticing when their recovery is improbable. Plaintiff's attorneys frequently forego asserting antitrust claims altogether and file state court lawsuits which assert common law tort claims, such as tortuous interference with advantageous

---

[32] Anderson v. Liberty Lobby, Inc., 477 U.S. 242 (1986); Celotex Corp. v. Catrett, 477 U.S. 317 (1986); and Matsushita Elec. Indus. Co. v. Zenith Radio Corp., 475 U.S. 574 (1986).

[33] 509 U.S. 579 (1993)

[34] See § 4 of the Clayton Act, 15 U.S.C. § 15 (2000)

[35] § 542.22(1), Fla. Stat.

business relations, arising from defendant's anticompetitive conduct. Such common law tort claims usually permit the plaintiff to recover punitive damages if the plaintiff can convince a jury that the defendant's conduct was willful and malicious.

By filing a claim asserting a common law tort claim in state court, the plaintiff can avoid the following burdens of suing for violation of federal antitrust law:

1.   Proof of market power.
2.   Proof of antitrust injury.
3.   The summary judgment standards of the "trilogy."
4.   If expert testimony is offered by the plaintiff, the reliability requirements of Fed.R.Evid.702.

Finally, lawsuits in state court often progress faster than lawsuits in federal court, and formal aspects of federal practice, such as the requirement of a written memorandum supporting or opposing a motion, are not applicable.

Exporting U.S. Competition Policy: Global Antitrust Enforcement. The Effect of U.S. Prosecutions of International Cartels on Worldwide Antitrust Enforcement.

During the past decade, the Antitrust Division of the U.S. Department of Justice (the "Division") has obtained billions of dollars in fines in criminal antitrust cases, including several fines exceeding $100 million. In 1999 alone, U.S. criminal antitrust prosecutions yielded $1.1 billion in fines. More than 90 percent of these fines were paid by foreign-based firms convicted of participating in international cartels.

The Division's high-profile prosecutions of international cartels created awareness among law enforcement authorities worldwide of the effective use of antitrust laws to identify and destroy cartel activity. Several foreign countries, including the United Kingdom, Canada, Brazil, Sweden, the Czech Republic, Switzerland and Denmark, adopted laws designed to prohibit and punish hard-core cartel activity. In addition, the Antitrust Division entered into antitrust cooperation agreements with enforcement agencies in several countries, including Australia, Germany, Canada, the European Union, Israel, Japan, Brazil and Mexico, to facilitate investigation and prosecution of international cartels. These agreements provide for exchange of evidence and assistance with antitrust investigative efforts. Several foreign governments amended their extradition treaties with the United States to include criminal antitrust violations.

Only ten years ago, the prospect that basic principles of U.S. antitrust law would be embraced so broadly and that worldwide cooperation in investigating and prosecuting cartel activity would occur so quickly seemed remote. These developments demonstrate that many foreign governments have recognized that business activities that they once tolerated as "business as usual" burdened their economies and inflicted serious economic harm on their citizens.

This accelerating cooperation among international antitrust enforcement authorities has tremendous significance to firms and individuals who conduct business in international markets. Firms must educate and train their employees about compliance with antitrust laws of all countries and jurisdictions in which they conduct business. Employees must understand the increased risk of detection of antitrust violations and the escalating consequences of multiple criminal prosecutions, including huge fines and enormous damage judgments for firms, and substantial prison terms for individuals.

The Division's Use of Cooperative Investigatory Tools

The Division has used its cooperative investigation agreements with foreign countries to gather evidence for use in prosecuting U.S. and foreign nationals. Division attorneys increasingly use two investigative tools in its investigations of international cartel activity. One is the execution of search warrants by foreign authorities on the Division's behalf to seize evidence abroad. In one investigation, over 100 German police officers assisted in the simultaneous execution of search warrants on multiple companies at locations across Germany.

Notably, few foreign countries have constraints on searches and seizures comparable to the limits imposed by the Fourth Amendment to the United States Constitution. Nor do many foreign countries observe limits on custodial interrogations or recognize a privilege against self-incrimination. Division attorneys argue that they are not restricted from using documents seized and statements taken by foreign authorities under circumstances which would preclude their use if obtained under similar circumstances in the United States.

Another tool that the Division has used in its antitrust investigations is border watches, which have resulted in detaining foreign executives when they enter the United States, serving them grand jury subpoenas and taking them before a grand jury to testify about matters under investigation. The Division has found that, when brought before a grand jury under these circumstances, foreign executives cooperate with its investigations more readily than their U.S. counterparts do.

Antitrust Enforcement in the European Union

European Union competition law bears some superficial similarities to U.S. antitrust law, but its derivation, goals and enforcement are very different than those of U.S. antitrust law. It is not necessary to describe those differences to state a few general propositions. First, EU competition law prohibits cartels and naked restraints of trade between competitors, especially price agreements and horizontal division of territories or customers. Second, EU competition law can be enforced in noncriminal proceedings by the European Commission ("EC"), which can and does assess substantial fines against firms which participate in prohibited agreements or practices.

Envisioning the Future

In the next five years, I would like to see the Robinson-Patman Act repealed, the antitrust exemption for major league baseball legislatively overruled, and the Sherman Act amended to increase to ten years maximum prison sentences for hard-core antitrust violations. Only the latter seems to have a reasonable prospect of being enacted.

Increase Maximum Prison Terms
Hard-core antitrust violations are simply a form of economic fraud. Yet, sentences for most fraud offenses are related directly to the dollar amount of the injury caused by the fraud. In contrast, the maximum prison sentence that an individual convicted of participating in cartel activity is three years, whether the economic harm caused by the violation was one thousand dollars or ten billion dollars. Some of the international cartels prosecuted by the Antitrust Division cost consumers billions of dollars. The prospect of a maximum prison sentence of three years, when the risk of detection is low and when recognition that the actual sentence will be

less than one year, has not been an effective deterrent. Increasing to ten years the maximum prison sentence for hard core antitrust violations would likely serve as a significant deterrent, particularly if the minimum sentence is linked to the dollar amount of the economic harm caused by the violation.

The current three-year maximum sentence is low, not only in relation to penalties for other forms of economic fraud, it is low in relation to other crimes which occasionally occur during grand jury investigations of antitrust crimes. When I counsel individuals before they give testimony to a grand jury, I explain that the maximum penalties for obstruction of justice and perjury are greater than for price-fixing or bid-rigging. I provide this explanation to emphasize that, if they are going to testify without immunity (which I would not permit), they would be better off admitting participation in an antitrust conspiracy than lying about it to the grand jury.

Overrule the Antitrust Exemption of Major League Baseball
In *Flood v. Kuhn*,[36] the kindest characterization that the author of the majority opinion could offer for the antitrust exemption for major league baseball was that it was "in a very distinct sense, an exception and an anomaly."[37] The author of the dissent described it as "a derelict in the stream of law that we, its creator, should remove."[38] No other professional sport enjoys antitrust immunity. No rational legal or economic argument can be made to support it. From time to time, committees of Congress have held hearings concerning the exemption, and several individual members of Congress and the Senate have threatened legislation which would remove it. Nevertheless, it has

---

[36] 407 U.S. 258 (1971)
[37] *Id.* at 281.
[38] *Id.* at 286.

survived more than eighty years of criticism and appears likely to survive for many more years.

Repeal the Robinson-Patman Act

The Robinson-Patman Act also stubbornly persists. The RPA continues to burden price competition in many industries, although "mom and pop" grocery stores had all but disappeared by the end of the third quarter of the twentieth century. Bills repealing the RPA have been filed several times, but none has garnered sufficient votes in committee to reach the floor of the House of the Senate. I suspect that the RPA will remain.

Key Pillars of Antitrust Lawyers' Success

Three factors are critical to successful antitrust practice. First and foremost is preparation. One must devote significant time reading cases, as they are decided, and current professional journals and law reviews. As lead counsel for a party in an antitrust case, you must learn and understand the facts. Many senior lawyers do not review "raw" documents, preferring to leave the drudgery to associates and paralegals. My view is that, as lead counsel, I *must*, and I do, review the documents, no matter how burdensome that is.

Effective communication with your client is crucial. The client must be advised of risks without sugar-coating them. The client must be advised about changes in plans and strategies, and receive regular reports of developments. The news is not always good, but communicating bad news is part of the job.

Preserving client resources is an important aspect of my approach to antitrust litigation. In preparing a case for trial, I economize wherever I can without compromising the client's interests. I once heard the general counsel of General Motors say: "Don't give me a five-dollar wedding when a two-dollar wedding will do." Antitrust cases are conducive to excessive discovery and unnecessary motion practice, much of which, in my opinion, is done to generate fees for lawyers. Some lawyers, unfortunately, abuse their clients' pocketbooks. They treat antitrust cases as gold mines – and they mine them to exhaustion. Clients do not make and sell products so that they can pay lawyers.

We attorneys would not exist if we did not have clients, and our fiduciary obligation to our clients is to serve their interests. Winning cases for clients is in itself a reward. When clients understand that you are trying to serve them and not yourself, they more willingly pay your bills, and they will continue to hire you to serve them. I consider practicing law to be a privilege, and I hope to enjoy practicing antitrust law for many more years.

Keith Rounsaville is a stockholder and Chair of the Antitrust practice group of Akerman Senterfitt, the largest law firm in the state of Florida, with offices in eight cities throughout the state. Mr. Rounsaville is resident in Akerman Senterfitt's Orlando and Tampa offices.

Mr. Rounsaville received a Bachelor of Arts degree with departmental honors from Yale University in 1967, and a Juris Doctor degree cum laude from Columbia University School of Law, where he was a Harlan Fiske Stone Scholar.

For approximately thirty years, Mr. Rounsaville has concentrated his law practice in antitrust litigation and counseling. He has been lead counsel for corporate clients in federal grand jury investigations of price-fixing or bid-rigging in multiple districts concerning school milk, water treatment chemicals, repackaged chlorine, metal building insulation and chain link fence. He also served as lead counsel for corporate clients in State of Florida antitrust investigations of price-fixing or bid-rigging concerning repackaged chlorine, pesticides and water treatment chemicals.

Mr. Rounsaville has served as lead trial counsel for plaintiffs and defendants in civil antitrust actions in the United States District Courts for the Middle, Northern and Southern District of Florida; Northern District of Georgia; Northern District of Alabama; Southern District of Indiana; Southern District of Texas; District of Maryland; and District of Colorado. His clients participated in many diverse industries, including pharmaceuticals, optical lenses, building products, citrus products, petroleum products, industrial chemicals, automotive products, and thoroughbred horseracing.

Mr. Rounsaville was ranked number one in antitrust practice in the 2003-2004 edition of Chambers USA America's Leading Business Lawyers. He served as Chairman of the Antitrust Committee of the Florida Bar for six years (1984-86, 1988-92) and was a member of the Executive Council of the Business Law Section of the Florida Bar for eight years (1984-92). He was elected to the American Law Institute in 1991. He is a frequent author and speaker regarding antitrust law, federal practice and procedure and federal evidence.

Mr. Rounsaville was admitted to the State Bar of California in 1971, to the District of Columbia Bar in 1972, and to The Florida Bar in 1974. He is also admitted to the Bars of the United States Supreme Court, United States Courts of Appeal for the Eleventh, Fifth and District of Columbia Circuits, and the United States District Courts for the Middle, Southern and Northern Districts of Florida.

Antitrust is not "Crumbs"

James R. Eiszner

Partner & Chair, Antitrust Practice Group,
Co-Chair White Collar Practice
Shook, Hardy & Bacon LLP

Not too long ago, I was contacted by the editors of this publication and asked to participate in this book by writing a chapter on my life as an antitrust lawyer. At the time of the contact, I was extremely busy – too busy, I thought, to accept the assignment. But then I recalled a scene from one of the great books of our time, Tom Wolfe's *Bonfire of the Vanities*. That book has nothing to do with antitrust law, but it does explain my motivation for writing this chapter. In the book, Tom Wolfe creates a scene in which one of the central characters, a bond salesman, is asked by his children what he does for a living. He is too busy with his chosen profession and too full of self-importance to respond to his children. The children then turn to their mother for the answer to the question about what the father does as a bond salesman. The mother duly punishes the father for his unwillingness to answer his children's question. She tells the children that bonds are like big loaves of bread that are transferred between rich people, that their father encourages the transfer of these big loaves of bread, and makes a living by picking up the crumbs that result from the transfer.

I do not want anyone to think that the practice of antitrust law is picking up crumbs. I have spent years practicing antitrust law and, while there have been some bumps in the road, have found it to be an extremely rewarding career. Perhaps no area of law is as intellectually challenging. I deal with a host of different industries and have needed to learn how those industries operate. I know how petroleum gets extracted from the ground, is converted to gasoline, and distributed to consumers. I have learned how writing paper is made, how new pharmaceuticals are developed, approved and marketed, how soft drinks are made and sold, how airline schedules are set, and even the ins and outs of distributing agricultural equipment.

Antitrust cases tend to be labor intensive. While most lawyers handle cases by themselves, antitrust lawyers need to create teams and make them work efficiently and cost effectively. As a result, I and other antitrust lawyers do not practice law alone. Many of my accomplishments are not really mine at all, but those of a team of lawyers which include me. Because I love teamwork, I have always found practicing antitrust law to be tremendously enjoyable.

One cannot understand what an antitrust lawyer does unless they understand what antitrust law is. It is not passing loaves to create crumbs.

The Basics of Antitrust Law

Hornbooks that teach the fundamental principals of antitrust law consume hundreds of pages. Lacking the luxury to devote innumerable paragraphs to explain basic antitrust law, I can only provide a brief overview and beg the reader's indulgence with a book review, rather than a tome.

Antitrust law can be defined in a single sentence. Antitrust law is the law that protects competition in order to maximize consumer welfare. But that sentence is packed with complex meaning. For example, what does it mean to say that the antitrust laws protect competition? It is perhaps best to define the protection of competition with drawing a distinction between the protection of competition and the protection of competitors. It is a fundamental tenet of antitrust law that protection of competition does not equate with protection of competitors. The competitive process is often brutal – good competitors dream of trouncing their rivals and, if they do so by introducing a better product or service or by achieving lower production costs and prices than their rivals offer or achieve, those rivals will be hurt severely. The rivals may find themselves driven from the marketplace because consumers do not want to buy their inferior or more expensive products. At the same time, however, consumers will benefit because of lower prices or better products. If antitrust law were to protect competitors, it would forbid a company from hurting its rivals by offering better or cheaper products than its competition would offer. But doing so would not maximize consumer welfare. The distinction between protecting competition and protecting competitors can perhaps be best understood by resorting to a professional sports analogy since sports involves competition. No one would complain if a professional athlete (or team of athletes) worked harder and longer than his (or its) rivals – yet those efforts to be superior would hurt those rivals, who might be defeated – or even humiliated – on the playing field. A rule protecting competitors, as opposed to competition, might limit how hard or long an athlete could work – and such a rule would hurt consumers (those who view the sport) by depriving them of the opportunity to see well-trained athletes. A rule protecting competition, however, would not hurt the quality of the athletic contest – for example, a rule prohibiting throwing games or outlawing alterations to standardized sports equipment (e.g., jet-powered running shoes, corked baseball bats, etc.). Like sporting rules, antitrust laws permit companies to compete, and thereby inflict wounds on their rivals, and in antitrust law, hurting a competitor is permissible as long as consumers benefit from the competitive process, typically through lower prices and/or greater quantity or quality of output.

It is also important to define the word "competition." In simple terms, competition is the process of making sales at the expense of others; such sales can usually be won only by providing cheaper or better quality goods or providing superior service. Antitrust law is concerned with preserving competition that is significant. In a broad sense, every product that consumers buy competes with every other item on which consumers can spend money; no one has unlimited sources of funds and every dollar spent on one product is money that cannot be spent on other products. Probably everyone has encountered a situation where they saw something in a store they would like to buy – perhaps an expensive clothing item – but they decided not to purchase the item because they needed to spend the money on something else they needed more – perhaps food, or housing, or life insurance. In that broad sense, expensive items of clothing could compete with food or life insurance, but that competition is not significant enough to be protected by antitrust law; the products are too diverse in nature. One customer who foregoes purchasing an expensive suit or dress may use the money saved to buy life insurance while another might forego purchasing the same clothing item in order to purchase an entirely different item, such as food. In general, significant competition between two products exists if the sellers of one product – perhaps a brand of mid-size automobiles – will adjust their prices in response to changes in the other product, perhaps another brand of mid-sized automobiles. It may seem intuitive that one brand of mid-size automobiles competes significantly with another until the concept of geography is introduced. For example, does a dealer selling a brand of mid-size cars in San Diego compete with a dealer selling the same brand of automobiles in Boston? In general, it is often dangerous to rely on intuition to resolve that kind of question. Antitrust law typically resorts to some sophisticated quantitative economic analysis to determine whether the pricing of one product responds to the pricing of other products and it is not possible to describe those analytical methods here.

Even the definition of the word "consumer" is subtle. In popular terminology, a consumer is an individual, as opposed to a company, who spends money. In antitrust terminology, the meaning is closer to the literal meaning – one who consumes (in the sense of using up, as opposed to ingesting). An individual who buys a carbonated soft drink for drinking is a consumer of soft drinks. A soft drink company, however, is also a consumer – of sweeteners, flavorings, carbon dioxide, aluminum (for cans), and plastic (for bottles).

Broadly speaking, in protecting competition, the antitrust laws govern two types of conduct: first, they regulate joint conduct, especially where two competitors are acting jointly, through some broad prohibitions; and, second, they regulate unilateral conduct in a narrow set of circumstances where the actor is a monopolist or near monopolist. In each case, the goal is to protect consumers by keeping prices low and output high.

With respect to joint conduct, the antitrust laws regulate conduct by competitors in terms of agreements with one another, for example, agreements to fix prices or allocate customers. Other joint conduct involving competitors addressed by the antitrust laws includes mergers and acquisitions (including joint ventures and strategic alliances) and boycotts (e.g., where competitors jointly agree they will refuse to deal with someone – for example, all the software companies agreeing they will not sell to any company who has been caught illegally copying software). Joint conduct involving a seller and a buyer is also regulated by the antitrust laws but with far fewer constraints than those that exist for joint conduct by competitors. For example, it is illegal for a seller to impose minimum resale prices on his customers; in certain circumstances, imposition by a seller of a requirement that the its customer resell the product only in a specific territory or class or trade can be illegal, as can a requirement that the customer refrain from buying from the seller's competitors.

The monopolization provisions of the antitrust laws apply to unilateral conduct by dominant sellers (companies that are monopolists or near monopolists). These provisions regulate the actions that dominant sellers can take if those actions are going to give them monopoly power, or increase their monopoly power, but importantly do not apply to prohibit the possession of monopoly power not obtained by improper means. A key test of legality is whether those acts improve consumer welfare. Antitrust law will not condemn acts that lead to the acquisition or enhancement of monopoly power through offering better or cheaper products: indeed, if a company made products that were far superior to what anyone else could make, one would expect that all consumers would want to buy those products. But if a company achieved or enhanced its monopoly position by burning down the plants of its competitors or by purchasing the entire supply of a key input when it could not possibly use all that it purchased, such conduct would be condemned as acts of monopolization under the antitrust laws.

There is a fine line between lawful competition on the merits and improper exclusionary practices, and often courts get confused about what is legitimate competition and what is not. Part of the problem is terminology – especially when some older decisions articulate the test as one of fairness. The antitrust laws do not and should not depend on some vague equitable notion of whether conduct seems fair or not. Rather, the critical issue is whether the conduct will enhance consumer welfare. The answer often depends on the particular facts of each case. For example, you could have a situation in which a company has monopoly power over one product -- every customer has to go to that company because it is the only source of supply. That company makes another product over which it does not have any significant power, but it says to all of its customers, "If you want our product which you can only buy from us, you also have to buy this other product we make, where we are one of several suppliers." And that practice could conceivably give them a monopoly position over that second product. If this arrangement actually threatens to create monopoly power over the second product, in most cases the arrangement will be illegal. But a slight twist in these facts can change the outcome. Suppose a gasoline company has developed a patented gas pump that it puts its trademark on. Because it has developed the gas pump and wants it to be used only at its stations, it tells the gas station owner that, if he wants to use the gas pump at his station, he has to buy his gas from that company. The patent may or may not give him a monopoly -- it may make him the sole source of that special gas pump which may give him monopoly power. In that case the company has a monopoly over the gas pump but faces competition in gasoline because there are other suppliers. Leveraging the gas pump monopoly by forcing users of the pump to purchase the company's gasoline could lead to a monopoly in the gasoline market. If so, the general rule would suggest that the company has engaged in unlawful monopolization. But under these facts, the company has an interest in seeing that only its gasoline is dispensed from the pump that has its trademarked name on it. Why? Because if the gas station were to purchase gasoline from another source and that gasoline was defective -- full of impurities because it has been lying around in the bottom of a tank somewhere -- when the gas station buys it, and it ruins the engines of all the cars into which it has pumped, the reputation of the company with the trademarked gas pump will be ruined. All of the customers who bought the bad gasoline will assume it came from the company because its name was on that pump and they thought they were buying gasoline made by that company. There are benefits to consumers being able to identify a product with a trade name (imagine how a consumer would feel it he or she entered a restaurant called MacDonald's and found that no hamburgers were sold by the restaurant). So there is an example where you could justify the conduct as enhancing consumer welfare: Under these facts, the monopolist's requirement that you buy his gasoline to sell through his patented gas pump is likely to be a permissible practice.

Antitrust law has other problems with terminology. The very definition of monopoly power is often a source of confusion. Older cases take the position that market power is the power to exclude competition or raise prices, while monopoly power is the power to both exclude competition and raise prices. This has led to perverse results: for example, someone who possesses a patent has the power to exclude anyone from practicing the patented invention which means that the patent holder also has some power to raise prices. Under the older formulations of monopoly power, a patent holder would always possess monopoly power. But this is nonsense – just ask most patent holders whether they are monopolists and they will likely inform you that their patented invention competes with many other products. Indeed, there are dozens of patents on common every day products like car parts and light bulbs – yet no rational person would find that there are dozens of light bulb or car part monopolists. The courts have come around to the position that the grant of a patent does not convey monopoly power. Yet, the courts have been slow to revise the definition of monopoly power to make sense. Compounding this problem is that in the field of economics, monopoly power and market power both connote the power to raise price above a competitive level. Under that standard, the number three car company (as well as the number one and two car companies) would be a monopolist -- it has some loyal customers who will buy its products even if they are priced a little higher than competing automobiles. Fortunately, courts have rejected the notion that there can be more than one monopolist in the market – after all, the word monopolist derives from the Greek word for one in the market. But even many of these enlightened courts have not come around to revising the definition of monopoly power. I think a truly enlightened court would define market power as the power to raise price above a competitive level and monopoly power as the power to set price without concern that others in the relevant market could expand output sufficiently to force a reduction in the price it sets.

Certain industries are more prone to antitrust problems. In terms of antitrust exposure for collusive activities, industries that are characterized by commodity products are very prone to antitrust problems. Industries that have somewhat differentiated products but who have a lot of foreign competitors, particularly competitors in jurisdictions that do not have antitrust regimes themselves, are often prone to antitrust risk. I think there are certain industries in the United States that are just not very popular, and plaintiffs will often select them not so much because there is a real antitrust problem in the industry but because jurors are not going to be very sympathetic to competitors in those industries. In that category I would probably include computers and computer software, pharmaceuticals, and perhaps automobiles. With respect to antitrust exposure unrelated to collusion, I think it is very hard to generalize that any particular industry is more prone than another to antitrust problems.

Practicing Antitrust Law

Antitrust is a very complicated, specialized, and evolving area of law. Consequently, an antitrust lawyer must stay on top of industry developments. The Internet has been a very big help in terms of allowing antitrust lawyers to keep abreast of everything in the field. I am now able to access daily what is going on at the Department of Justice, at the Federal Trade Commission, and at the European Union Competition Directorate without leaving my desk, so I can stay up-to-date on new developments. The court system has also developed electronic internet access, which allows you to access dockets via the Internet. You can find actual pleadings in cases, at least in federal court and in many state courts, and that has allowed me, for example, to put in a request: what were all the antitrust cases filed in the country today? And you can get an answer to that query, and this helps keep you abreast of developments.

There are also the information services that report on antitrust decisions, and I try to stay current with those. Another important information source is the antitrust community in general. Antitrust typically involves multiple party plaintiffs and multiple party defendants, and you make a lot of friends and acquaintances from being involved in those cases, and you can stay in touch with them and discuss what is going on in the industry and what new decisions are made and what is the significance of the new decisions and so forth. And, of course, when you have clients who are large enough to have law departments that have antitrust lawyers, you talk to those lawyers all the time about new developments as well. That helps you stay on top of what is going on within the client company as well as in the antitrust community generally.

One great piece of advice about practicing antitrust law was actually from an adversary whom I greatly respected. He always said that if you have to try an antitrust case with more than a hundred documents, you should give up because you are going to lose. I always thought that was great advice. Antitrust law tends to be extremely complicated, and judges and juries can and do get lost with complicated things. If it takes a lot of documents and testimony to persuade a judge or jury, they will not be able to deal with the complex story you are trying to tell. Consequently, I have always operated on the principle that it is important to simplify. Application of that principle is not limited to the court room; clients and sometimes even co-workers need to understand the advice or instructions that are being given.

To be successful as an antitrust lawyer, you need to know the facts and the law and the economics better than your adversary. Some kinds of antitrust cases are relatively straightforward. Because there is no defense or justification for conduct such as price-fixing, the issue is a straight factual issue: did the company engage in price-fixing or not? But in cases where the conduct is not *per se* illegal (i.e., indefensible), the issues can be extremely complex and often require sophisticated economic analysis presented through economic experts. An antitrust lawyer must be able to understand the economic theory as well as the expert, to discern whether the expert's economic testimony is consistent with the applicable legal standards and the facts of the case, and to make it clear to a court or a jury – most of whom have had little or no economic training – that the expert does or does not have a credible opinion on the issues in the case. This is only possible if the lawyer truly understands economics, antitrust law, and the facts of the case.

I also think that credibility as a trial lawyer is important for antitrust lawyers. Perhaps more than any other area of law, antitrust cases are "bet the company" matters for defendants. Not many cases get tried and there are some antitrust lawyers who have never tried a case – or have tried a case but only poorly. Whether representing a plaintiff or a defendant, a lawyer who does not have a track record of trying and winning an antitrust case will cost his client money. Your adversary will know that your client is unlikely to let you try the case – few clients will risk a high stakes trial on the success of a lawyer who has not tried big cases before – and that knowledge will permit your adversary to insist on a trial absent a highly-favorable settlement for his or her client. On the other hand, if you do have credibility as a good trial lawyer, your adversary will usually not want to face you in court and will be quicker to settle. I have had a few situations where opponents have voluntarily dismissed my client from a case because they did not want to try a case against me. I am not suggesting, however, that I have won every case or intimidated every opponent. I have lost cases and think that losing some cases is an important, though unpleasant, learning experience. A good deal of my personal motivation to win for clients comes from the desire to avoid the unpleasantness of losing.

I believe what separates the great from the good is not only knowing the law and the economics and the facts, but also having a great deal of common sense and the ability to think strategically by putting oneself in the other person's shoes, thinking about how he is going to react, and planning a response to that reaction. I have always believed this is very important and, even when my adversary strikes a particularly effective blow, I look for the opportunities that he or she has provided me by striking that blow. There is opportunity even in adversity. Good judgment is also important: you are often making judgments about the risk of losing which requires making judgments about a jury's ability to understand the facts or the court's ability to grasp a fine distinction. If you make a mistake in judgment, it can cost your client a great deal of money.

Preparing a Case

In assessing a potential antitrust case, the first thing I want to identify is the conduct. There are some types of conduct that simply cannot be justified – for example, price fixing. If the client has engaged in that conduct, or has arguably engaged in that conduct, you want to find out the facts. If they did engage in that conduct, I think the best thing to do would be to encourage them to try to obtain an appropriate settlement, and, failing that, to litigate the case. In these situations, litigation only happens when the litigated judgment is the most appropriate settlement because the other side cannot be objective about its case in the settlement process. When the conduct can be justified, however, you have to find out what the reasons for the conduct were, and make sure that the conduct is actually justified by those business reasons, and then start to show the world that those justifications are real and substantial, and outweigh any anticompetitive effects of the conduct that is in question.

You would most likely have to have witnesses who would be able to show that they took this conduct for the following business reasons, and that the business reasons are legitimate and not after-the-fact rationalizations. There may be situations in which you can find someone else engaged in this conduct, whether it is a competitor or someone facing a similar problem, and this company has taken similar actions and thinks the conduct is reasonable, and it would be helpful to have their testimony saying this is how this problem ought to be handled. In almost every case, you want to bring in an economic expert who will look at the conduct from the perspective of economic theory. Remember that most of antitrust law is dependent on economic theory. The expert would explain to the jury how this is the only reasonable way – or at least a very reasonable way – to proceed when the client is faced with these business problems or has these business needs. And, of course, you would also need probably an economist or perhaps an accountant who can deal with issues on damages, in case you lose on your justification.

My preference is to select the experts early, but experts can be an expensive component of the cost of litigating, and clients are sometimes resistant. Consequently, the first job is essentially to convince your client, if he or she needs convincing, to hire an expert fairly early in the game so that you understand all the issues that the expert may have – after all, those issues may also be issues that the other side has identified – and deal with them to make the best case possible for justifying the conduct. Once you have thought personally about the justifications and your defenses in light of the evidence and talked with your expert about what he or she sees as the issues, then you need to go out and develop the facts and probe your witnesses, usually with your client, to see whether their business justifications are consistent with what the economist and you see as the justification. If so, you want to do all that you can to ensure that the witnesses sing that song loudly and consistently with other witnesses. You obviously cannot ask any witness to lie, but you do want to try to make the story as consistent as possible, while adhering to the truth at all times.

Evaluating Risk for Clients

Risk assessments are important both to counseling clients on proposed conduct and to advising clients in the litigation context on whether to accept a settlement or proceed to trial. Antitrust cases are expensive propositions just to litigate and get more expensive if you lose. It is critical that an antitrust lawyer be able to assess the risk that a proposed course of conduct will result in an antitrust case being filed. It is perhaps even more important to be able to assess the client's prospects for prevailing in an antitrust case once one has been filed.

In terms of counseling, you first want to have a good understanding of the conduct that is proposed, the business objective that the conduct is supposed to achieve, and the nature of competition in the industry that could be affected by the conduct. Once you are comfortable that you have the necessary understanding, then you start to discuss and evaluate with the client whether the proposed conduct is likely to be challenged if undertaken, and, if so, who would likely claim that they are harmed by the conduct if it were undertaken. You need to determine whether the claimant is likely to be a competitor or a customer or a supplier. If it is a competitor, an important principle to keep in mind is that competitors tend not to complain about anticompetitive acts. They tend to complain about acts that make them have to compete even harder than they are now. So you need to ascertain whether the competitive complainant is going to complain for a legitimate reason (i.e., that competition in some way would be adversely affected by the proposed conduct), or whether he is really complaining that he now has to compete harder because of the conduct that is proposed.

If the claimant is likely to be customers or suppliers, you need to explore with your client why he or she wants to undertake actions that hurt the company's suppliers or customers. After all, these are people that he or she does business with. I always tell my clients that I do not particularly like it when they try to practice antitrust law, and they should not like it particularly well when I try to practice business. So I just ask them to think through that process. Sometimes they have not; often they have. And then you try to get a sense of whether the business justifications are likely to outweigh the anticompetitive effects, and if it is likely that the justifications will be outweighed by the anticompetitive effects, you need to explore with your client whether there are other, more lawful ways – or at least less questionable ways – through which they can achieve their business objectives.

There are a few clients – although I think it is fairly rare now – who basically do not care about complying with the antitrust laws. They want you to bless their proposed conduct, and they will tell you anything that will lead you toward that conclusion, even if it is not supported by the facts. It is important that a lawyer and a client trust each other. If you have a client that you are somewhat concerned about and in whom you do not have a lot of trust, you need to document the underlying facts and make sure that this is not a rush to judgment – that the proposed conduct is really lawful before you tell them that it is really lawful, and that is always a big challenge.

Another challenge is the fact that some of the competitive effects that you need to consider can be very expensive to explore. You need to make a judgment as to the market in which the client competes. In litigation, that is typically resolved by subpoenaing lots of companies who are arguably competitors within the market, getting their data, using your data, having an economist analyze the pricing and output data, and making a determination as to what the relevant market is. That can be an exercise that can cost thousands if not hundreds of thousands of dollars. And for a business proposal, clients sometimes resist efforts to try to make precise determinations of the competitive effects. At that point, there is a cost-benefit analysis. How well can you really assess this market without all the economic data? If you think you can make at least a reasonably educated judgment as to how the economic analysis would likely turn out if you conducted it, then you go forward; if you cannot make an educated judgment, you need to tell the client that they really ought to spend the money if they want to eliminate the risk. But even then there is a cost-benefit analysis, because sometimes the competitive concerns caused by the proposed conduct are so small that it is just not even worth doing a full-blown economic analysis; you could bless the transaction right up front without doing all that. So you have to try to balance the cost of counseling with the need for the information and the benefits of having accurate advice.

Risk assessment in the litigation context is different. It requires making judgments about a jury's ability to understand facts and the judge's appreciation of the nuances of antitrust law. A lawyer should always be confident in the case he intends to try: it is impossible to get a jury to believe your version of the facts if you do not express confidence that you believe your version of the facts is correct. There is always a danger that the lawyer's confidence in his or her case clouds the lawyer's judgment about how the jury or the judge will likely find the facts. Some of the largest antitrust verdicts have come because the defense lawyer handling the case was not able to step outside his or her role as litigation counsel and make an objective assessment of what the jury or judge was likely to believe. When I advise a client on my objective assessment of the risks to trying a case, I always try to dial back my confidence in my ability to persuade the jury or the court so that I do not give my client an inaccurate, overly optimistic view of the chances of success.

Recent Changes in Practicing Antitrust Law

Antitrust law is constant evolving. Because it relies so much on economic theory, antitrust law changes as economic theories change. Antitrust policy also used to change with political administrations, depending on whether the party in power was pro-business or anti-business. Administrations that were against business brought cases hoping to achieve changes in antitrust principles that hurt the development of business, while pro-business administrations sought to do the opposite. But this is becoming somewhat less significant as the courts have relied on economic learning, and less on political philosophy about whether business is good or bad. Now, political philosophy tends to affect antitrust only at the margins. Political administrations no longer try to change legal principles; they accept the current state of the law and worry about how aggressive to be prosecuting cases on the facts. Anti-business political administrations tend to be more willing to bring cases that factually are less certain of winning under the current state of the law while pro-business administrations will bring cases that are more likely to win. I do not see any political administration trying to change how the law is interpreted in the future.

One of the trends I have noticed recently is that courts have become more concerned with clearing their dockets, and this has caused courts sometimes to certify classes in class actions, not because the law says certification should be granted, but because the court believes that if they certify the class, it will force the defendants to settle and the case will get off their docket. I think that has long been a problem, but the recent emphasis of the judiciary on disposing of cases has exacerbated the problem. Class actions should be certified when they are a just and efficient way to proceed; they should not be certified just because the coercive nature of a class action as a practical matter will require the defendants to settle, thereby removing a case from the court's docket and making the court appear to be efficient.

I have also seen a trend among the courts in antitrust law involving price fixing, primarily, and a few other areas. There is a doctrine called the "direct purchaser rule": only the purchaser who bought directly from the company or companies that engaged in the price fixing can recover under the federal antitrust statute. A few state legislatures (about a third of them) have passed laws that say you can also recover even if you are not the direct purchaser. In other words, you bought from someone who bought from someone who bought from the price fixer. That development has had the impact of greatly increasing risk on defendants. And then, in addition, some courts have said, "I don't like the federal rule, and I think the ultimate consumers who bought the product, rather than the first company in the chain of distribution, ought to be able to recover, and even though I have plaintiffs in states that don't have indirect purchaser laws, I'm going to invent some equitable theory on X that will let me circumvent the federal law ban, and the state law ban, on having indirect purchasers recover for antitrust violations." That approach has put enormous pressure on the defendants who now have to litigate in multiple forums and have multiple risks of liability. Even a company who is absolutely innocent cannot run the risk that it can repeatedly convince jury after jury of its innocence: it has to settle. Of course, settlements and adverse verdicts have to be paid – typically by each defendant raising prices on products sold in the future. So customers get an antitrust award but have to pay higher prices in the future as a result. At some point, our legislatures need to think about whether laws that increase antitrust liability exposure – either by expanding the universe of permissible plaintiffs or by providing that damage awards are multiplied (e.g., treble damages) really benefit anyone other than the plaintiffs antitrust class action bar.

More generally, there have also been changes in economic theory that have impacted antitrust law. In the last ten years, antitrust law has imported from economics the "unilateral effects doctrine" for merger analysis which has brought about a sea change. We have also had improved data handling capabilities due to the speed and capacity of PCs and so forth, so you can now manage data much better and apply doctrines such as the unilateral effect doctrine much easier. I have seen a rise in the use of some very sophisticated antitrust economics, particularly in litigation or investigations that involve the government agencies, and I think that will eventually spread to private litigation. But I have a concern that juries are not going to understand the sophisticated economic analysis, and maybe down the road we will have a situation in which juries decide antitrust cases not on the expert economist who has the best and most appropriate analysis, but based on who has the antitrust economics expert who seems like the nicest person. We may need a specialized antitrust court so that antitrust cases can be decided in a just and appropriate manner.

Technology has also affected the ability to handle some of these cases, just generally. I think e-mail has been terrific. I know when I started practicing, you would get involved in an antitrust case that involved multiple defendants, and suits in multiple jurisdictions, and just keeping everyone coordinated and informed of all that was going on could take the full time of several lawyers. Today, with e-mail and Internet-based document management programs and so forth, you can keep everyone informed with one part-time person. I see that as an improvement; it has helped to drive down the cost of litigating antitrust cases somewhat, and I think it will continue to do that.

In terms of trends, the government's amnesty program on the criminal side has also been significant. Years ago – going back to the 1950s – if you engaged in price-fixing, it was a misdemeanor not much different from a traffic ticket in the United States. Congress subsequently made it a felony, and people could go to jail, so clients started to take antitrust compliance more seriously. Recently, Congress has passed laws that have increasingly raised the fines for criminal antitrust liability. So losing a criminal case can be very expensive financially for the defendant, even putting aside the monetary costs of disposing of the follow-on civil actions that are likely to be brought. The Justice Department has very cleverly come up with an amnesty program that basically says the first company that self-reports with information about which the government did not already know will get amnesty and will not be prosecuted for its conduct on the criminal side. There will still be some civil liability. That program has caused a marked rise of people running in to the Justice Department and self-reporting involvement in antitrust activity. That is good for enforcement, but it has also, I think, caused clients to be extremely serious about self-policing themselves. I expect that trend will continue as the agencies convince Congress to increase the criminal penalties for antitrust violations making the amnesty program even more attractive. Other countries are developing antitrust laws or have had them, and they have noticed what has happened in the U.S. experience, and now they have started to raise the penalties for antitrust violations and have amnesty programs themselves. So you find situations in which someone self-reports in the European Union, and that leads to antitrust litigation and antitrust investigations in the United States, because there is coordination between many of the antitrust enforcement authorities around the world.

The Future of Antitrust Law

In the future, I would like to see a couple of things happen. One, in price fixing cases, this indirect purchaser rule where the cases are brought into state court and then direct purchasers can sue in federal court – I would like to see someone rationalize that kind of litigation, because it really does put defendants in a situation where there are too many things to coordinate and too much risk, and cases are not decided on the merits (i.e., did the client engage in illegal conduct or not?). They are often decided on how much of a nuisance and how much risk a plaintiff can create, given the inability of courts and juries to deal with the complicated issues involved in antitrust cases. So I would like to see something done to get the government enforcement agencies to pursue collusion claims on behalf of direct and indirect purchasers and worry about how it is allocated between the two of them later. At the present, there is no allocation. Such a change can only be achieved if Congress steps in and revises the whole regime of private remedies.

A related development I anticipate is a change to the law awarding treble damages to a civil antitrust plaintiff. Originally, a private plaintiff could get three-fold its actual damages for injuries caused by a violation. The theory of awarding treble damages was to encourage private plaintiffs to supplement the government's antitrust enforcement efforts by bringing cases which the government did not pursue. But that theory generally has not held. Private plaintiffs generally file suit only where the government has pursued a case. It makes no sense to reward the private plaintiff who sits back and lets the government develop the antitrust case. At a minimum, Congress should amend the treble damages provisions so that a private plaintiff's damages are trebled in cases where the government has not investigated the defendants' conduct that is the source of the private plaintiff's injuries. It would be wise for Congress to make this change before some court holds that the antitrust regime is unconstitutional. Currently, we have a system where for a single antitrust violation, the government can obtain a criminal fine of up to double the damages caused by the violation; purchasers who have bought directly from the violator can treble damages, and indirect purchasers can get treble damages under state antitrust laws – usually for the very same overcharges on which the government's fines and the direct purchasers' damages are based. In other words, a defendant is punished for his antitrust violation by being required to pay eight times the actual damages it inflicted. In the context of punitive damages, the Supreme Court has said that requiring a defendant to pay eight-fold the actual damages caused would be unconstitutional. At some point, a court will decide the scheme of antitrust remedies is also unconstitutional.

In the merger area, I see a movement toward trying to rationalize all the various antitrust regimes that exist around the world. At present, a large international acquisition is a logistics nightmare, requiring premerger notification filings in sometimes dozens of jurisdictions, each with a different substantive standard for assessing the lawfulness of the merger. In the United States, the basic inquiry on a merger is whether the merger is going to make consumers better off or worse off. That is true in some other jurisdictions around the world, although they may differ in how they analyze a merger to determine whether consumers are better off or worse off. The European Union, in addition, has a slightly different standard; they do look to see if consumers are better off or worse off, but they also worry about it impacting trade within the common market, which is a different standard. And then there are some countries whose antitrust regime is basically "we don't want any mergers that are going to result in closing of plants and loss of employment in our country." The need to make numerous premerger notification filings and to justify a single acquisition under different standards for legality makes it very costly and I have seen situations where the cost of notifying and justifying a proposed merger is so large that it makes it uneconomic for clients to pursue mergers that would actually benefit consumers if they could go forward. I think the antitrust enforcement agencies are starting to realize that the existence of multiple filing requirements and multiple merger enforcement standards is hurting the very consumers that the agencies are meant to protect. As a result, the antitrust enforcement authorities in the U.S. and the European Union have at least explored ways in which to make this process a little bit saner by working to develop a single merger notification system. That is not yet a reality but it will be soon. There has also been a movement among antitrust and competition lawyers worldwide to get what is referred to as convergence – to get all the antitrust merger regimes to converge and use the same standard. It has been a positive global development. There is some talk of trying to get antitrust regimes to converge generally – not just with regard to mergers but with regard to all conduct. Given issues of sovereignty for each nation, I do not see that happening. I think it is a utopian dream of some of my colleagues.

In the future I think it is possible that specialized courts will be established to deal with antitrust matters. Antitrust, as I have said, depends heavily on economic theory and economic analysis, and that analysis and theory is becoming much more sophisticated. It is very difficult for judges who have five hundred cases on the docket and only one or two of them are an antitrust case, to take the time to specialize in economic theory and antitrust law and as a result, many bad decisions issue. I would like to see Congress pass a law to authorize specialized antitrust courts, so that we can have judges who are able to devote the time to learning the economic theory, or at least specialize because they have enough cases that it makes it worthwhile for them to specialize in antitrust. Right now the laws are so diverse and often complicated – we ask many of our judges to master an incredibly diverse number of special legal areas, and sometimes they are not always able to do that. Because antitrust policy often derives from antitrust case law and because the decision of an antitrust case can affect an incredible number of interests not represented by the parties in the antitrust case itself, there is good reason for Congress to take steps to insure that antitrust cases are correctly and intelligently decided.

James R. Eiszner chairs Shook, Hardy & Bacon's Antitrust and Trade Regulation Practice Group and co-chairs the firm's White Collar Practice. Mr. Eiszner is a graduate of Princeton University and New York University School of Law, where he was also Articles Editor for the Review of Law and Social Change. Before joining the firm, Mr. Eiszner practiced antitrust in New York for twenty years where he was a member of the Antitrust and Trade Regulation Committee of the Association of the Bar of New York City.

Mr. Eiszner is a trial lawyer who has tried both civil and criminal antitrust cases to successful verdicts. He also has successfully tried administrative proceedings before the Federal Trade Commission and has a successful track record in defending preliminary and permanent injunction cases brought by the federal antitrust enforcement agencies, by state attorneys general and by private parties seeking to prevent consummation of mergers. He also regularly consults with clients who seek counseling on antitrust matters.

Mr. Eiszner advises clients on all facets of the antitrust laws, including pricing and distribution issues, mergers and joint ventures (including premerger notifications), patent licensing, standard setting, trade association activities, consent decree compliance and antitrust exemptions. He has designed antitrust compliance programs and participates frequently on antitrust and compliance presentations to business people. He has been retained by various investment houses to advise traders on the likely outcome of antitrust challenges to proposed mergers.

The Fundamentals of Antitrust Law

David A. Ettinger

Chair, Antitrust and Trade Regulation
Honigman Miller Schwartz and Cohn LLP

The Basics of Antitrust Laws

The antitrust laws are designed to protect the process of competition and to prohibit activities that interfere with that process. It is the process that is protected rather than any particular firm. In the competitive process, firms may be injured or destroyed. That does not raise antitrust issues unless the injury results from activities that harm the competitive process.

There are a number of antitrust statues at the federal level. Every state with the exception of Pennsylvania has its own antitrust law, and most foreign countries have antitrust or competition laws as well. In general, the antitrust laws prohibit conspiracies in restraint of trade – that is, conspiracies that harm overall competition. They also prohibit mergers and acquisitions that have the potential to create that harm. They also prohibit some single firm conduct, though they are more limited in that regard. The federal antitrust laws prohibit single firm conduct that monopolizes a market or creates a dangerous probability of monopolizing a market. Leveraging a monopoly in one market to harm competition in another market may also be prohibited. Finally, some state laws also prohibit actions that may be in their incipiency but have a potential to cause the same kind of competitive harm.

One misconception concerning the antitrust laws is that many people feel that the antitrust laws protect them against hard competition. It is quite clear that hard competition is to be desired under the philosophy of antitrust laws, and therefore, for example, low pricing without more is not unlawful except in limited circumstances.

There are a number of different kinds of antitrust cases. One category, of course, is private litigation brought by private parties. The other kinds involve government regulators; at the federal level, the Department of Justice and the Federal Trade Commission both pursue antitrust matters. The Justice Department pursues criminal antitrust matters exclusively. The FTC today pursues certain kinds of industries more commonly than the Justice Department. For example, the FTC tends to look more at healthcare issues than does the Justice Department. The Justice Department tends to be more involved in computer software matters.

Increasingly, the states have become involved in antitrust issues, and many state attorneys general have people working on antitrust issues full time. An antitrust lawyer always has to be aware of the states in which his client's conduct is occurring. The involvement of state enforcement officials may vary depending on the kind of industry affected, and whether the behavior in question tends to be localized. State attorneys general have often gotten together and brought cases on a national basis. Sometimes the state attorneys general are more interventionist in their philosophies than the federal regulators.

Susceptibility to an Antitrust Issue

In assessing an antitrust problem, the first thing to examine is the conduct itself and whether the conduct could restrain competition, e.g., limit the ability of sellers to effectively compete or buyers to have access to a number of sellers. Activities such as agreements on price, agreement not to compete, agreements that foreclose competition (such as exclusive agreements), or mergers that eliminate competition are among those kinds of conduct that can raise antitrust issues. Even if the conduct is potentially anti-competitive, in many cases that is not enough. You then have to look at the impact on the market in question. You have to define the market first and then decide whether the market overall will be harmed by that conduct. If not, in many cases there is no antitrust problem. In other cases, an antitrust problem and an anticompetitive effect are presumed because the conduct is of a kind that is viewed as almost always being anticompetitive. That analysis applies to such activities as price-fixing between competitors and agreements between competitors to divide up markets between themselves.

There are certain kinds of industries that are highly competitive and where there are no or very limited barriers to entry. In those industries, it is very difficult for conduct – no matter how badly intended – to have an adverse impact on the overall market. For example, retailing is in many ways an area in which there is a lot of competition, and there have been relatively few antitrust problems found with respect to retailing over the years. There have nevertheless been some cases in particular kinds of retailing where antitrust problems have been found. The Staples/Office Depot merger involving office superstores was successfully stopped by the FTC; the agency convinced the court that there was a separate market for office superstores and in that market, there were very few competitors and therefore there was a concern. A number of supermarket mergers have been enjoined over the years.

At the other extreme, markets with few competitors and high barriers to entry are the kinds of markets in which antitrust problems are more likely, and those are markets where there has been a great deal of antitrust activity. Again, the likelihood of an antitrust problem may depend on the characteristics of competition for a given product at a particular period of time, but antitrust concerns have been common in certain high-tech markets in recent years. The characteristics of the market often lead to one or two winners and a lot of losers. If there is conduct in such a market that can restrain competition further, that can be especially significant.

The Role of the Antitrust Lawyer

I am a general antitrust lawyer and I do the full range of things that antitrust lawyers do, including litigation, counseling and dealing with government investigations of both conduct and, specifically, mergers and acquisitions. I can come in contact with a client under many different circumstances. If a firm is sued and it needs a lawyer to defend it, its personnel may call me. If a firm's personnel believe that it is being harmed in an anticompetitive way in the marketplace, either as a customer or a competitor, they may talk to me and determine whether it makes sense for them to sue or to complain to the government. If a firm becomes a subject of a government investigation, its personnel may call me. Clients who are involved in mergers or acquisitions between competitors or, under some circumstances, between buyers and sellers, may call me to see if I think there is going to be an antitrust issue and if they need to prepare for questions from the government about whether their merger is anticompetitive. Finally, clients will call and just say, "I want to do X. Is X a problem under the antitrust laws? Do I need to change what I want to do?"

One of my jobs is to inform clients of the antitrust risks from particular conduct. That usually involves providing a judgment, not an objective, certain answer. The antitrust laws, of course are very technical and you can usually find support in the case law for many propositions, including sometimes contradictory propositions. It is also true that antitrust problems are usually fairly complex factually. The answer will frequently depend not on some simple legal rules but on an analysis of a particular market and what you think is going to happen in that market. What a good antitrust counselor needs to be able to do is synthesize the facts and the law and not be afraid to make a judgment despite the presence of uncertainty.

One principle I emphasize to clients is that they need to look at the antitrust issues relating to a course of conduct sooner rather than later. Sometimes antitrust issues become an afterthought after a plan is already launched. In that event, it can be difficult to take all the steps to plan properly and minimize the antitrust risks. Antitrust matters are often fairly large and fairly complicated, and in that sense they become chess games, and you need to think pretty hard about what is going to happen several moves down the road.

A related challenge in the antitrust area is being able to balance the need for information with the client's expectations in terms of time and costs. There are pitfalls in both directions. It's always great to get more information, but when the client wants an answer, one thing you need to do is decide how much expense it wants to incur for that answer and then try to accommodate it. At the same time, it is also sometimes tempting to give a quick answer without really understanding the marketplace, and that can easily lead to errors. The antitrust lawyer has to weigh those two considerations and try to provide the best answer possible within the client's constraints.

One mistake an antitrust lawyer can make, potentially, is to rely too much on a client's decision-makers. That's because the people at the top of large corporations, in my experience, rarely have very good information about the detailed issues that are critical to an antitrust lawyer. An antitrust lawyer really needs to understand the details of how a market works. Many very smart CEOs, when I interview them and ask them these questions, give me answers that I later learn – through looking at detailed documents and talking to people in the trenches – are incorrect because the CEO operates at a more general "high level." An antitrust lawyer should not hesitate to say that he needs to talk to other people and learn what they have to say; the boss may not know it all.

Key Skills of a Successful Antitrust Lawyer

An antitrust lawyer needs to understand economics. To do that well, an antitrust lawyer needs to be mathematically fluent as well, since economics depends on math. Lots of people go to law school because they don't like math or science. It's surprising how many antitrust lawyers are not comfortable in these areas. That is a real handicap – first, because you need to understand the economic issues underlying antitrust problems, and second, because antitrust cases depend much more than many other cases on expert economic testimony. If you are going to shape your economist's work and undercut the other side's economist, you had better understand what they are talking about and understand it thoroughly so you are not just along for the ride.

Beyond that, an antitrust lawyer needs an ability to tell a story and communicate, as every lawyer does, but the difference is that an antitrust lawyer has to be able to do so with respect to matters that often involve uniquely complex legal and factual issues. This is, of course, critical because if a judge or jury doesn't understand the issues you've developed, they are irrelevant. Very few judges, including federal judges, have significant antitrust backgrounds.

A good antitrust lawyer also needs to have management skills. Antitrust cases tend to be so large that often there are significant teams of people working on them on either side, and you have to be able to cost effectively manage a group of lawyers, who are often not the most manageable of people. Antitrust cases need to be both artistic successes and financial successes.

Mergers and Acquisitions

If a client wants to acquire another company or be sold to another company, the first step in the process is to understand the position of the companies and the kind of market they are in. The standard antitrust questions about market share, barriers to entry, and relationships between buyers and sellers must be addressed. This will involve interviews with many knowledgeable personnel and review of the documents that have been created by the client to describe the market, including strategic plans, and also documents describing the merger. These documents potentially can be very helpful to your case or a smoking gun against your case. This process is often complicated by the fact that at the early stage when you are starting to evaluate a transaction, usually the transaction is extremely confidential even within the company, and there may be a limit to the people you can talk to and documents you can see without compromising confidentiality.

The next step is advising the client what the likelihood is that the transaction will go through. What is the likelihood that there will be a serious investigation? How will that impact the timing of the transaction and its costs? Antitrust investigations of mergers can result in what are called second requests and can go on for many months. That can have a serious impact, for example, on a company that is being sold if it is known in the marketplace. Customers may not want to deal with a company being sold, and key employees may start to leave. And if the transaction ultimately fails, the selling company can be in serious trouble. The failure can hurt it far more than the purchaser. The client needs to understand these business risks in deciding whether a transaction should be attempted.

The rest of the process occurs after the transaction is announced. A filing is made with the government if the transaction and the parties are of the requisite size. There are then two kinds of issues which must be addressed. The first involves responding to the government's request for information and documents; that can be quite massive. Often hundreds of boxes of documents need to be gathered and produced, sometimes from all around the world. The second involves making your case to the government as to why the transaction is not anticompetitive and why they ought not to challenge it and why if they did they would be beat in court. Both of those activities are going on with the clock running very fast, and it is a very intense process.

The process of opposing a merger is different. One can sometimes sue to prevent a merger. That is both very expensive and often faces legal obstacles. A competitor has to tell a fairly specific kind of story in order to have standing and be able to claim antitrust injury to oppose a merger. The antitrust laws suggest that under many circumstances, though not all, mergers that are anticompetitive will help other competitors in the market, because they will result in higher prices and that will benefit all the competitors. The people who are typically more frequently harmed by an anticompetitive merger are customers. While customers in theory could sue to stop a merger of their suppliers, it does not happen very often. Customers can be understandably reluctant to go to war with their suppliers. They may also not have enough at stake to justify the kind of expense that is involved.

What is more typical when a party wants to oppose a merger is to simply go to the federal agency or state agency that is looking at the merger and try to convince them that they ought to stop it. You can also provide them with information that they can use to stop the merger and provide people who can testify in court.

In the merger context, an antitrust lawyer needs to think about not merely what the judge would want to hear, but first what the regulators are interested in, which is often more technical and more sophisticated. You also may need to address confidentiality issues, because your client may be very concerned that the news will leak that it is opposing the transaction, and that can cause it problems in the marketplace later. I have had cases in which clients had some interest in opposing a merger but decided that the risk to them in the marketplace – if someone figured out that they were opposing it – was too great and they decided not to go forward.

Preparing for Trial

An antitrust case is different from some other types of litigation in a few respects. First, cases tend on average to be bigger and be more complicated. There are often very significant issues of document production and document control and expense – and how logistically to even review and analyze the documents that are produced when you are talking about very big corporations. The issues are also more technical. One challenge in an antitrust case is that it works on several levels. There is the technical level of assessing economic evidence, undercutting the other side's expert testimony and developing your own. Then there is the level of trying to boil this down and explain to the judge (who might hear three antitrust cases every five years) what it is all about. Then the challenge, ultimately, if the case goes to trial, is to explain the case to a jury. Thus, an antitrust litigator has to be able to handle very technical economic issues but at the same time be able to adequately describe them in simpler terms.

Antitrust cases are very fact intensive – more so than many other kinds of cases. The key is really understanding how the particular marketplace at issue in the case works. I often view an antitrust case as having two parts of the case. The "who did what to whom" part of the case – what was the conduct – and then the effects issues. Part of the reason I am an antitrust lawyer is that I am much more interested in the effects questions. The effects questions are unique to an antitrust case. Even if the bad things or the supposedly bad things were done, did it matter to the marketplace? Did it cause damages, and how do you analyze that? That is the technical area of the case.

Reaching a Settlement

As in any case, a settlement depends upon an assessment of the risks of trying a case, the cost of settling, and what you give up, and that is a very individual process in each case. I have found that because antitrust cases are big cases and because the remedies are usually very significant, the case rarely settles at the first attempt. If a case settles, it is usually well down the road after the court has decided not to grant summary judgment and it is clear to the defendant that it faces a serious risk. There are usually several "minuets" prior to that time where the parties talk and fail to agree because the defendant still hopes to settle the case cheaply. On the defense side, a fair number of antitrust cases are dismissed fairly quickly because many cases are simply not very good.

Changes and Trends

The most significant change in the antitrust laws today is probably the growing importance of economic analysis. An outsider might think, "Of course economic analysis is important, because it's all about economics," but the antitrust laws until the late '70s reflected a set of populist principles that didn't apply a lot of detailed economic analysis. The importance of economics in antitrust has grown steadily since that time and has really become critical to a great deal of antitrust jurisprudence. In the end, if you are not thinking hard about the economic principles involved, you are not really looking at your case properly.

Another major change is the globalization of antitrust. Today, almost every country in the world has an antitrust law, including countries that have only recently begun to adopt market economies. In many locations, antitrust regulation is as significant as in the United States. When you are involved in transactions involving major companies that operate beyond the borders of the United States, then you always have to worry about not one set of laws but often many sets of laws.

To the extent that there have been differences in the application of antitrust or competition laws, those differences are narrowing. Not very long ago there was a vigorous discussion about the differences between European competition laws and U.S. laws, and I think we are already seeing in reaction to that controversy that the enforcement philosophy in Europe is becoming more similar to that in the U.S. I think we will probably end up with a set of antitrust laws that at least in the developed countries will be fairly similar around the world.

One thing that may or may not happen, though we are headed slowly in that direction, is that as economics becomes more sophisticated and as more empirical work is done, all the premises of the antitrust laws will be examined. For example, one basic premise, under the antitrust law, is that higher market shares result in markets being less efficient and prices being higher. We may find over time that even that fairly basic presumption is wrong in some industries. That kind of issue is being looked at, and hopefully it will be looked at more over time. Antitrust is nothing if it is not based on facts that we learn about how markets really work. It is important that the antitrust laws keep evolving in light of what we know.

David Ettinger is a chair of Honigman Miller Schwartz and Cohn LLP's Antitrust and Trade Regulation Department. A 1976 graduate of the University of Michigan Law School with graduate level training in antitrust economics, Mr. Ettinger has spearheaded the firm's antitrust practice for twenty years.

Mr. Ettinger's activities include the litigation of major antitrust cases, including both private cases and cases brought by federal and state antitrust agencies, as well as advice and counseling on antitrust and trade regulation issues for clients in a wide variety of industries.

Mr. Ettinger has served as lead antitrust counsel in a number of antitrust cases of major national importance. These include Hassan v. Independent Practice Associates (the leading case on HMO and network antitrust liability), United States v. Mercy Health Services (successful defense of a hospital merger against a Justice Department challenge), Compuware v. IBM, (challenge to monopolization of mainframe software products) and the successful defense of a number of antitrust class actions. Mr. Ettinger was one of the pioneers in developing defenses to "indirect purchaser" class actions brought on behalf of consumers.

The Benefits of Antitrust Law

Michael Sennett

Chair, Antitrust and Trade Regulation
Bell, Boyd & Lloyd LLC

The Basics of Antitrust Law

Antitrust law is a set of business laws designed to promote competition and reward synergies, efficiencies and technological advances. At their source, the antitrust laws in the U.S. advance consumer welfare by preserving the benefits of the process of competition for customers specifically and the economy more generally. These laws are not intended to protect individual competitors or the weak or inefficient. Competition is paramount and if there is "cheating," if a business or businesses working together adopt practices that keep prices artificially high or restrict customer options in the marketplace, the antitrust laws will step in to prohibit the anticompetitive practice and return the market to a fully functioning free market.

In preserving the rule of competition, the antitrust laws ensure that our precious and scarce resources are allocated effectively and efficiently. Waste is eliminated and unearned wealth transfers based on restraints are eliminated. If a business is not performing well – if it is inefficient, if it has lazy managers, if it is being mismanaged, or if it uses old technologies – our antitrust laws will protect the process of competition which will ensure that underutilized resources are redeployed and more efficiently used and allocated. Thus, antitrust law is designed to reward and promote innovation, new products and services and more efficient processes.

It is the economic underpinnings of antitrust that control much of the thinking in the courts today. Given that the process of competition should produce better products and higher quality at a lower cost, all to the benefit of the customer, courts focus increasingly upon the consumer return from vigorous antitrust enforcement and are less concerned with insulating competitors from the ravages of "ruinous" competition. As a general operating principle, if a company truly is in business to serve customers, and genuinely puts its customers first, that company will rarely, if ever, have antitrust issues arise from its strategies and practices. If what a company does genuinely enhances customer welfare, its actions will ordinarily be defensible under the antitrust laws.

Of course, although a company may be successful in developing a product or services on its own merits – it is truly superior to its competitors – such company does have responsibilities under the antitrust not to abuse that market power, or dominant position, as it is called in Europe to acquire or maintain a monopoly. If company "willfully" uses its market power to stifle competition, innovation or technology advances to the long-term injury of U.S. commerce, the antitrust laws will step in to protect customers against such conduct and "level" the competitive playing field.

The role of the antitrust lawyer in the U.S. is to understand these principles thoroughly and to assist clients in developing business strategies consistent with them. Being too conservative, or denying clients market opportunities because of an unschooled fear or risk aversion under the antitrust laws, can be as or more damaging to consumer welfare than letting a close question strategy play out in the market. The evaluation of strategy opportunities, business plans, venture proposals, marketing programs and mergers and proposed demand of the antitrust lawyer, complex risk assessments and judgments without easy rules to follow. Much of antitrust law falls within the subtleties of a gray zone, and the skills antitrust lawyers bring to bear are designed to educate clients in risk assessment and to develop in them sensitivity to nuances of competition principles. At bottom, our task is to guide clients toward successful implementation of strategies that are consistent both with their business plans and with the antitrust laws. We act as strategists first and foremost, and then as prosecutors or defenders following implementation of strategies in the marketplace.

There are several different areas within the practice of antitrust law. Antitrust lawyers can counsel (and defend the practices of) clients in mergers, acquisitions and joint ventures and in licensing, marketing, distribution, pricing and the patent and technology antitrust interface. Antitrust lawyers represent clients before regulatory agencies and the antitrust enforcement agencies, as before grand juries for criminal antitrust matters and in court for civil and criminal antitrust matters.

Antitrust Counseling Strategies and Methodologies

The scope of an antitrust practice in the U.S. can be very broad from active counseling to long trial work in the courts. In the first instance, we are antitrust advisors and act to use and interpret antitrust law and economics in a very positive way with clients. We strive to have them understand what it is, how it affects their business decisions and how they can make plans and strategies consistent with it. Antitrust compliance programs, proactive antitrust education and antitrust audits are effective in helping clients understand antitrust, making it second nature in their business decision making and avoiding litigation. Clients need to understand that antitrust litigation is extraordinarily expensive (primarily because of the complexity of the factual arguments and the cost of producing and examining what could be tens or hundreds of thousands of documents for any given case), and an essential role for the antitrust counselor is directing the client in developing systems and practices that will evaluate antitrust risk and to avoid or reduce the likelihood of antitrust litigation, all without harming the robustness of the business itself.

As antitrust lawyers, we do our very best to be creative, to think outside the box and offer solutions that meet the client needs with as little antitrust risk as possible. We seek advice from or cooperate with enforcement agencies when we need to, and work through problems aggressively so that the company does not face unnecessary antitrust risks that go to the heart of its business. Unfortunately, antitrust litigation too often does put much at risk for corporations – often their very method of doing business is challenged – so the premier challenge for antitrust lawyers is to develop business solutions for problems that accomplish the company's business objectives consistent with the antitrust laws.

The strategies change with each transaction and in each industry; every situation demands a unique set of solutions. Antitrust law as applied remains extremely fact intense and advice can change instantly with any change in facts. Service industries versus manufacturing industries or traditional industries versus new, emerging industries – each market has its own competitive dynamic which directly impacts antitrust strategies and advice. As antitrust lawyers, our first responsibility is to learn the business thoroughly so we can customize our approach. An attorney who wants to practice antitrust law should be prepared to learn the clients' business inside and out. That rule applies to every business, every market and every industry. Depth of knowledge and a range of experience with a clients' business is critical to an effective assessment of an antitrust problem.

Litigation and Government Investigations

Government cases usually start with an investigation. Private litigation may start with warning letters or often the preemptive filing of a lawsuit. Antitrust investigations and lawsuits can continue for five, ten or fifteen years. The discovery process is quite lengthy and burdensome. Because often a business practice is at stake, a case may involve the production of almost every document generated regarding the business – sales, pricing, marketing, financial statements, manufacturing records, licenses, distribution agreements, supply arrangements, business plans – over a period of several years. It is expensive and takes a time to gather documents, negotiate scope of documents to be produced, review documents and focus on the crux of the case. Discovery can be very disruptive to the company and the costs involved can be staggering. Antitrust litigation is not lightly invited nor lightly embarked upon.

Settlement processes in antitrust cases, which sometimes involve different skill sets than litigation, are also more complex than the settlement of more straightforward commercial cases. Settlements that may require changes in business practices, sales of a division, etc., offering of coupons or rights and the evaluation of alternatives takes time. In cases initiated by the government, the government may stay involved as a monitor for some time, even after the case has been seemingly settled.

It is also important to assess antitrust risk early in litigation and to continue assessing it, constantly making judgments for the client about litigation strategies for dealing with antitrust exposure. Some cases are systemic – a case that challenges the basic way a company does business. Others are conduct driven – say, a conspiracy case to fix prices or allocate territories with competitors. Were the acts committed or not. Often, antitrust litigation will touch other aspects of the business. A company may need to defend itself in some particular way because the implications of the antitrust challenge go beyond the immediate litigation.

When cases begin with a government investigation, the antitrust lawyers works very hard to address the government's concerns. This process often includes providing detailed explanations to the government about business practices, perhaps a white paper getting deeply into facts and documents. Generally, for the client the commencement of a government antitrust investigation will also trigger an internal investigation for the client.

Antitrust litigation recognizes that there generally is more than just money involved; many antitrust cases result in injunctions and fundamental changes in business practices. Antitrust cases are about how your client conducts its business. The theory of the defense case will rely quite heavily on what is reasonable. The theory of the prosecution will depend on showing the business practices at issue and how they hurt purchasers and consumers. At bottom, were the challenged practices good for customers and consistent with consumer welfare. Antitrust litigation starts with everyone's theory and then builds the facts that develop the case. Certainly, if the challenged conduct is alleged conduct that the client does not believe occurred, a defense is built upon an intense investigation of past conduct.

Because of its complexity, as law and facts, the first and foremost rule for antitrust litigation is simplify, simplify, simplify. The case, whether for the prosecution or the defense, has to be understandable and believable, whether it goes to a jury or to a judge. Themes are essential. Making 200 points even though there will be 200 points to be made can run counter to this rule. Judgments and assessments in litigation about what arguments and facts are most important, and how they can be made understandable, requires risk taking. Key is to focus on what risks to take that are more likely to assure a win, and for the defense to win before the case goes to a judge or jury. Defendants will assess many avenues that might terminate a case early. We examine whether these are the proper antitrust plaintiffs. We look at jurisdictional issues. We look at whether there could be antitrust injury or antitrust standing deficiencies. Because it is an antitrust case and because it is large litigation and expensive, we tend to examine virtually every procedural issue to determine whether and when the case can be won and how to minimize the expense and disruption to the client's business. A keen sense of judgment is vital in antitrust litigation – particularly in helping the client to assess the merits realistically and in evaluating the cost benefit of each litigation decision.

Mergers and Acquisitions

The most effective way to counsel a client on the antitrust aspects of a proposed merger, acquisition or joint venture is to work with the client from the very inception of the deal. Working with the clients on antitrust strategy includes asking the critical questions – how is the transaction viewed internally, what is the likely market and customer reaction, what is to be said about the reasons for the transaction, what is the financial and competitive analysis of it, what documents will be generated and what benefits are expected. If the client waits to engage antitrust counsel until the transaction is signed, it is often too late to undue the damage caused by troublesome documents, financial assumptions, market share analyses and the like. Too often, absent antitrust input, the assumed business reasons for a transaction are not carefully considered and may be at cross purposes with the antitrust laws. Poor choices of words or faulty pro forma may costing the transaction days, weeks or months in delay as the enforcement agencies work though their analysis. In some cases, neglecting early antitrust counsel in an antitrust sensitive transaction can make the difference in a close competitive analysis and cost the client the transaction.

When antitrust lawyers approach an M&A deal they first assess the markets and market shares for a "quick look" to determine whether a proposed deal may have antitrust risk. We ask questions up front to elicit very targeted information. How concentrated is the market? How big is the deal? How will consumers be impacted by the merger? Who will complain about it? Is it a global deal? In Europe? In the U.S. only?

For larger transactions, a Hart-Scott-Rodino Act filing, a European Commission filing and other regulatory filings may be required and a series of waiting periods observed before the deal closes. Often governmental enforcement agencies request additional information about the market and the client's business before the deal is permitted to close. These questions can add many months to the timetable of a transaction. The client may have to make adjustments to the deal or assess settlement, divestiture and litigation options. Antitrust lawyers may have to make the client's case to the government, demonstrating how this deal is good for customers by detailing the synergies and efficiencies that are created by combining certain businesses. The strategy for each transaction will be tailored to fit the issues it raises and the given market circumstances it presents.

Training Antitrust Lawyers

The training process within the antitrust bar to develop a skillful antitrust lawyer is longer than for many other lawyers, largely because the size and the complexity of antitrust matters take time to work through. As a result, it takes many years for someone to develop into a capable antitrust lawyer. There are two principal training paths – government enforcement agencies (the Federal Trade Commission and the Antitrust Division of the Department of Justice) and private practice law firms. Most positions with the government agencies are in Washington, D.C. Antitrust positions with law firms tend to concentrate in Washington, D.C., New York and approximately 10 to 15 other major cities. State antitrust enforcement agencies tend to seek already experienced antitrust lawyers and also tend to have very few antitrust positions even in the largest states.

In training new antitrust associates, a heavy emphasis is placed on teaching the basics of antitrust law and economics. We want them to learn the law thoroughly as a first step. There are some antitrust laws, like the Robinson-Patman Act, which address niches of antitrust law and can be arcane and difficult. The law is learned by research and study, working on the background antitrust analysis for client counseling or litigation projects. This continues for the first several years, along with the simultaneous development of litigation skills.

Antitrust is not a practice for lawyers who want to try a lot of cases. Associates who want trials right away and who crave lots of experience in court would be disappointed in antitrust, which in practice has a heavy litigation component without necessarily getting to trial. We have new lawyers do some smaller, general litigation cases for the trial experience, always emphasizing skills development. Associates work on teams, and they might often find themselves as number four or number five on a team for the first several of years, and then number three or number four on the team for the next several years after that. They build experience, and some do take responsibility more quickly than others.

We spend a lot of time on the mechanics of skill set development, setting up courses, teaching, writing, taking our associates through as much of the antitrust process as is possible. But I also tell the new lawyers to think about this as a long-term commitment to an area of practice. It is not something you do well as an adjunct to lots of general litigation or corporate work. Either you do it with full commitment, or you should leave it to others.

Keys for Success as an Antitrust Lawyer

Because of the size and complexity of the antitrust practice, from counseling to litigation, most antitrust law is practiced in the U.S. in the government or in larger law firms. A case of any consequence requires large groups of lawyers, often with a wide array of individual expertise. Some lawyers have more experience with criminal grand juries, perhaps being ex-antitrust prosecutors themselves, and have a focus on the criminal side – a price-fixing case, for example. A vertical distribution civil case would present a different set of issues and require other expertise. In high technology cases, intellectual property lawyers may need to be involved. Thus, with the myriad of skills involved, antitrust law remains largely the province of larger firms or specialty antitrust litigation boutiques, which themselves still have some size and scope.

Practicing antitrust law is detail oriented and requires a great deal of diligence and hard work. At the same time, to do it well requires something of a strategic and philosophical outlook on business enterprises and the markets within which they operate. You also have to be something of a visionary in the way you think about and solve problems, with a genuine premium placed on "thinking outside the box."

To be successful, you must develop an ability to conceptualize quickly and to solve clients' problems with business solutions. That requires a great deal of empathy for the client's business people and business drivers. A successful antitrust lawyer can usually – not always, but usually – accomplish all of a client's objectives, although it might be in a different or unexpected way. That's the challenge of antitrust counseling: You may need to show a client a different way of doing something that will result in the client accomplishing most or all of its objectives. You want to show the businesspeople that to execute a proposed strategy, for example, they do not need to sacrifice the points they deem important, which could range from their customer communications, to their internal practices, to the way they run factories.

Working well with the facts, understanding what's important, is essential for an antitrust lawyer. Judgments are based upon facts and assumptions, and clients will keep coming back when they realize that your judgments are sound and their interests come first. They need to hear harsh judgments, for example, when a case or conduct is sadly all but indefensible. They need to hear sound judgment on when to settle and when to litigate, with their interests put first. Law firms fail with their clients when they pursue the big lawsuit on a "scorched earth" basis when it is at the expense of sounder judgment on the expense of litigation and the risks of nonsettlement. Litigation at all costs is a great driver of profits for law firms, but it is a poor substitute for a business judgment in the antitrust field. Clients will keep coming back if they trust and believe in your antitrust advice through their own experience with you.

Practicing antitrust law is very much a lifestyle choice for a lawyer. Antitrust is truly the essence of business, its strategy and pursuit of clear victory. Antitrust lawyers learn what makes a business go, its marketing aspirations, its sales goals, its new products, its competitive strategies. The practice itself requires long hours and can be physically very demanding. But because it involves very directly the very business of the client, it will be important to the client and generally will demand priority.

Because the antitrust lawyer learns the business inside and out, there is quite a bit of travel involved. You go to the client's place of business, get to know the major players and understand not only how the business operates and its place in the market, but why. As a result, it is exciting from a personal development standpoint, and antitrust law remains a very vital practice -- rarely boring and often surprisingly fun.

Biggest Challenge: Take the Law Seriously

The biggest challenge faced by an antitrust lawyer is to convince potential new clients to take seriously the consequences to their business of ignoring the antitrust. Too often businesses follow what other companies do or what they believe they need to do to survive or prosper. Once an industry faces a massive antitrust prosecution, it will be forever changed. Our key challenge as antitrust lawyers is to convince clients to change before the antitrust enforcement action – with all of its costs and consequences – arrives. Often the most antitrust compliant clients are those who have suffered through a prior antitrust prosecution. Our challenge is to educate clients in the experiences of other clients so they will not have to suffer the burdens of a prosecution.

An antitrust lawyer counsels clients to think about antitrust and how the concepts embodied in the antitrust laws can be consistent with their business practices. Many of the companies that have learned to incorporate antitrust law concepts into their practices remain successful in their business. We need to have clients think about antitrust law along with tax and securities law, disclosure issues, environmental issues and the whole panoply of legal matters they face. We advise them not to put antitrust too far down their priority list, because if the government comes calling it inadvertently could become the number one priority for all the wrong reasons.

Types of Industries More Prone to Antitrust Problems

The industries that are more prone to be confronted by antitrust problems tend to be those with the highest-profile – our most important industries. Industries with dominant players and industries with a tendency to cartel activities also attract antitrust attention. Healthcare and telecommunications generally are prone to antitrust problems arising from the complex markets within which they operate and the myriad of arrangements and players that are in place. The pharmaceuticals industry and all of its facets is an important subset of healthcare for antitrust purposes. Any industry with high-cost or high-risk patented products will draw antitrust attention. Information technology is an industry faced with important antitrust problems. Finally, energy more generally and the newly deregulated industries tend to be more prone to antitrust problems.

The markets in most of these industries tend to be very large and antitrust misbehavior is quite costly to the economy. Some of these industries are highly innovative but are tending toward consolidation because size and scope bring so many synergistic advantages. These consolidations tend to be subject to more comprehensive antitrust review among the enforcement agencies.

Misconceptions

The largest misconception in the business community is that the antitrust laws are there to protect competitors. Many believe that any time a competitor gets injured in the rough and tumble of the marketplace, the antitrust laws are not far behind. There is a general sense that somehow weaker or smaller or more thinly capitalized competitors ought to be protected against the process of competition.

Another misconception is that the antitrust laws unfairly penalize the highly successful companies, for example, like Microsoft. Sometimes businesspeople – not those who were suffering from Microsoft, but those outside the industry – view an entity like Microsoft as the epitome of success, and believe that the antitrust laws are being used to punish them for succeeding.

Antitrust laws do not punish success; they reward success. They punish conducts that denies competitors an ability to compete on the merits of their products, services and skills. It is the use, or abuse, of market power that the antitrust laws rain in. Market power as a concept factors into antitrust frequently – both positively when used for customers' benefit, and negatively when used to injure competition. But it is competition that is most important – the process of it – not the individual competitors. When one company has substantial market power, its competitors may suffer, but it is the reduction of customer options as a result that is the true concern of the antitrust laws.

These misconceptions may not remain long term. A gradual understanding has emerged that the antitrust laws serve consumer welfare and are not there for the protection of competitors. It is a recognition that is developing more slowly in Europe, where the Commission and the courts give a lot more weight to competitor complaints as it did in the General Electric/Honeywell matter.

The antitrust law has developed some in denying competitors much of an ability to challenge anticompetitive conduct. The principal champions of the antitrust laws are those who suffer when competition fails – the customers. If the customer does not feel aggrieved, then neither should the competitor, who may be limited in its ability to bring an antitrust case.

Antitrust will remain a complex area of law for business; it is difficult to summarize in sound bites. Clearing up public misperceptions about it is largely an educational process, and it will not get cleared up very easily or very quickly. More business education will help – going to clients and putting on seminars for their business development people and strategic planners.

Many of those at the top of companies, the CEOs and other C-level executives have worked with the antitrust laws and in antitrust matters over time and view it as a positive experience. What they do learn is how to think about their business, how to write about their business, how to conceptualize their strategies, and how to think through their customer goals. Antitrust law gives them a great understanding of key business drivers, and the lawful limits of strategic conduct.

Recent and Future Changes in Antitrust Law

The principal recent change in antitrust law has been its globalization. Ten years ago 98 percent of merger filings, merger review and antitrust law matters were U.S.-based only; as a practical matter, except for the very largest global transactions, the United States was the only jurisdiction that mattered, even for transnational transactions. Today, we often spend as much time with antitrust issues developed outside the United States as we do with those in the United States, particularly when the European Union is involved.

At last count there were more than 90 jurisdictions and sovereignties with some form of regulatory antitrust principles in place with additions each year. Although 40 to 50 or so of these locales are neither enforcement-oriented nor have well developed antitrust laws (and the markets of the nations themselves may not be very significant on a global basis), many of today's mergers and related work will require antitrust review in 20 or more jurisdictions. This brings a whole new complexity to the antitrust practice. It has been a phenomenon driven largely by the European Union and much of its recent merger work. And in other areas – such as cartel activity – the U.S. government and the European Commission are challenging global cartels developed, maintained and located off-shore.

Today U.S. grand juries reach into conduct that occurred in Switzerland, in Argentina or in Singapore, and as a result we find ourselves having to take a much more global view of what we do. What is common in these jurisdictions is an enhanced emphasis on antitrust economic principles. Economics has become a much larger focus because it is what all antitrust laws have in common. There are variances and intricacies in every set of laws, but what they do have in common, in a genuine antitrust regime, is the basic industrial organization economic principles that are applicable across the world.

There has been a great deal of debate on where antitrust law is heading globally. The United States has weighed in a few times, probably more often opposing the globalization of antitrust law, for example under the World Trade Organization, and this opposition has resulted in much debate over the character of antitrust globalization. It appears to be principally heading toward an increased emphasis globally in stopping cartel activity, largely price-fixing, group boycotts and market allocation conduct.

We will continue to experience an active governmental interest in the review of horizontal mergers, which are mergers among competitors, and we will continue to see occasional but serious enforcement against abuses of dominant position, such as the Microsoft-style investigations and similar activities. These three areas, cartel-enforcement, merger review and a few monopoly cases, will fuel the growth of antitrust worldwide, and antitrust enforcement likely will be focused upon whatever industry is hot at the time.

There was a lot of discussion about e-commerce two, three, four years ago in the antitrust bar, and today we spend much less time with it. That does not mean the principles are not applicable there; it is simply that the business activity has moved on, and antitrust moves with it.

The increased interplay of intellectual property and antitrust law has changed how we approach antitrust law. I think there has been an emergence of interest in recent years; it is an active legal specialty in the United States and around the world. Intellectual property protection is a priority of many, many companies; they depend on it for their value and their livelihood. It used to be that antitrust, at least in the United States, was hostile to and would routinely trump patent law, but that has changed significantly. The interplay of those two is still hand-in-hand, and we work closely with intellectual property lawyers on matters that cross our two areas of practice.

Antitrust law will continue to be important when addressing licensing, strategic joint ventures and special partnering arrangements – the sorts of arrangements that are less than mergers and acquisitions, but more than purchase and sale agreements between companies. Many such undertakings are driven by technology sharing, patent licensing, and trade secret arrangements. In Europe new "block exemptions" must be considered as well as changes in antitrust enforcement in the United States in this field, and these intellectual property law developments are changing what we do as antitrust lawyers.

Finally, I think another principal change we will see in the practice of antitrust law is that the practice will tend to be a focus at fewer and fewer firms but with larger and larger competition law practices, all driven by increased specialization and concentration, which is probably the trend of the practice of law more generally.

I do foresee antitrust as a robust practice for a number of years to come. It is ingrained as an area of law the understanding of which is essential to any company that wants to be successful. Over the next ten to fifteen years, we will see an increasingly active government antitrust enforcement effort directed at cartel conduct, and it will use nontraditional law enforcement and investigatory techniques. We will see more sophisticated conspiracy investigations than we have historically, and we will probably see it trending toward increased cooperation internationally among enforcement agencies.

The real challenges for the antitrust lawyer over the next 10 to 20 years will be to remain on top of the rapid changes in legal and economic thinking on antitrust law, to continue to develop and refine risk analysis for clients, to approximate a science and to ensure that our own resources are properly allocated to respond to antitrust demands on a global platform. Antitrust lawyers will need to know their clients businesses at their fingertips to be able to respond more quickly, more immediately with judgments clients will trust and follow.

There is also some room for true reforms in the antitrust practice. Most immediately, simplifying and staging the antitrust process with the government or in private litigation would result in much sharper, much more coordinated challenges to various business practices. Both merger and acquisition antitrust matters and private litigation need to be streamlined in some effective way without losing the essence of the analysis. We produce massive amounts of underlying documentary material in discovery or a merger review that is rarely if ever dealt with in most antitrust cases. What is also out of control is the process of dispute resolution through the courts when multiple forums vie for different parts of an antitrust matter, until it becomes a procedural morass of conflicting challenges, with claims and court rulings inconsistently layered one upon another on the same antitrust point. Much has been written on the Microsoft case in this respect. But anything that would simplify the fact-finding process and more quickly separate the real antitrust cases from the unsupported cases would be welcomed by both the business community and the courts and would be a genuine positive change for the process of practicing antitrust law.

Michael Sennett, a member of Bell, Boyd & Lloyd LLC, chairs the firm's Antitrust and Trade Regulation Department and serves on its Management and Executive Committees. His practice is concentrated in antitrust and trade regulation law with an emphasis on the antitrust aspects of mergers and acquisitions, international transactions and joint ventures and matters before regulatory and antitrust enforcement agencies as well as in the courts and before grand juries. He also provides counsel on pricing, distribution, e-commerce, advertising, marketing, technology licensing, patent-antitrust and related trade regulation matters and regularly handles a broad range of antitrust and business litigation in courts throughout the United States.

Mr. Sennett serves as antitrust and trade regulation counsel to a number of multinational companies, investment banking firms, trade and professional associations. He is admitted to practice before the U.S. District Courts for the Northern District of Illinois (where he is a member of the Trial Bar) and the U.S. Courts of Appeals for the Second, Fifth, Seventh, Eighth, Ninth, District of Columbia and Federal Circuits and the United States Supreme Court.

Mr. Sennett serves as an adjunct law professor at Loyola University Chicago, where he teaches international antitrust law, and is a member of the Board of Advisors of the Institute for Consumer Antitrust Law Studies.

He received his A.B. with high honors from Quincy College and an M.A. from Northwestern University. He received his J.D. cum laude from Loyola University Chicago School of Law, where he served as Executive Editor of the Loyola Law Journal.

Practical Aspects of Antitrust Law:

What Every Business Executive Should Know

James J. Calder

Partner

Katten Muchin Zavis Rosenman New York

Antitrust Law – What It is and Why It Matters

It is an article of faith in the United States that we have a "free market economy." Unlike socialist states that intensely regulate their economies, the United States tries to let the forces of supply and demand regulate its markets. This belief, that the "magic of the market" does a far better job of allocating resources than government regulation, is a cornerstone of American economic policy. Indeed, the American reliance on free markets instead of government regulation is frequently viewed as one of the primary reasons for the great resilience and strength of the American economy since the end of World War II.

Antitrust law is the vehicle used to protect American markets and ensure that the free market economy on which American prosperity is based is in fact "free." Antitrust law does this by forbidding certain conduct – such as price-fixing, bid-rigging and market allocation – that defeats the competitive process. It also seeks to protect markets by regulating the merger process to ensure that, after a merger, a sufficient number of firms remains in the affected markets to provide meaningful competition. By protecting the competitive process and the competitiveness of American markets, the antitrust laws help ensure that purchasers of American products and services (both consumers and businesses) enjoy the benefits of low prices, high quality, constant innovation and rapid response to the changing demands and requirements of the buying public. The role of antitrust is so important in protecting the U.S. economy that the United States Supreme Court has referred to the Sherman Act[39], the primary antitrust law, as "the Magna Carta of free enterprise."[40]

---

[39] 15 U.S.C. § 1 et seq.
[40] United States v. Topco Assocs., Inc., 405 U.S. 596, 610 (1972).

For the business executive, the antitrust laws present a code of conduct that must be respected and followed. That code is so important that hard-core violations are prosecuted as felonies with individual violators regularly being sent to prison and corporate violators paying fines in the hundreds of millions of dollars.[41] While these are serious obligations imposed on every enterprise that does business in the United States, the antitrust laws also provide real and vital protections for the business community. For example, just as the Sherman Act forbids a business from conspiring with its rivals to fix prices, that same law protects that same business from price-fixing by its suppliers. Thus, the antitrust laws prohibit firms from subverting the competitive process while simultaneously protecting them from injury resulting from the subversion of that process by others.

It is sometimes perceived in the business community, and in some business publications, that aggressive antitrust enforcement is regulation run amok.[42] In fact it is just the opposite. In the United States, antitrust is the antithesis of government regulation. The theory of antitrust is that the economy works best when markets are free – when they are open and not restricted by anticompetitive activities or anticompetitive strictures. When markets are open and competitive, the need for economic regulation is minimized. Confusing antitrust enforcement with government regulation is thus a serious mistake. In the absence of aggressive antitrust enforcement, the norm would likely be more government regulation, not less.

---

[41] *See* R. Hewitt Pate, Testimony Before the Committee on the Judiciary, U.S. House of Representatives, Concerning Antitrust Enforcement Oversight, July 24, 2003, *available at* http://www.usdoj.gov/atr/public/testimony/201190.htm (discussing multi-million-dollar criminal fines and prison terms imposed against executives of such companies as Sotheby's auction house, Hoechst A.G., Akzo Nobel Chemicals B.V., Elf Atochem, and Arteva Specialties S.a.r.l.).

[42] *See, e.g.,* Holman W. Jenkins, Jr., *FTC Screams for Antitrust*, WALL STREET JOURNAL, March 11, 2003.

The Role of the Antitrust Lawyer

In a general sense, the role of the antitrust lawyer is like the role of the lawyer in any area — to protect his client and further his client's interests. In the antitrust context, however, this frequently requires more than just defending a case, responding to a government investigation or shepherding a transaction through the merger review process. Frequently, representing a client in an antitrust matter requires modifying or defending fundamental aspects of the client's business model. This is a role that lawyers in other areas of practice rarely face. For antitrust lawyers it is fairly common. For example, antitrust issues regularly arise in connection with the methods by which firms distribute, sell and price their products, bundle their products for sale, license their technology, and interact with their competitors. The resolution of these issues requires that the antitrust lawyer develop a real understanding of how the client's business works and be able to work with the client in fashioning antitrust solutions for the client's antitrust problems that protect its business model and make commercial sense.

The antitrust lawyer has an additional obligation that is also rarely found in other substantive areas of legal practice. As mentioned earlier, the antitrust laws protect clients from the anticompetitive conduct of others. The antitrust laws thus always provide a business client with protections as well as obligations. Helping a client understand that antitrust may be a useful tool (or weapon) in dealing with competitive problems is a crucial aspect of the antitrust lawyer's role. For business clients used to dealing with government law enforcement matters from the standpoint of responding to a government inquiry or plaintiff's complaint, the notion that antitrust can be a useful tool in pursuing one's business strategy may be new and in some cases surprising. It is essential that the antitrust lawyer make his client aware of this other and potentially powerful side of antitrust.

Given these somewhat unusual roles played by antitrust counsel, it is vital that the antitrust lawyer develop a real understanding of his client's business. The best antitrust lawyers understand their clients' businesses well enough that they can help craft antitrust solutions that not only provide antitrust protection or solve antitrust problems, but that also make business sense. For antitrust lawyers, more than those in other areas of the law, truly understanding the client's business and what works and does not work for the client is vitally important. Lawyers who can combine their legal skills with an understanding of what the client needs to do to make his business work effectively, and the creativity to craft solutions that meet both antitrust and business requirements, can do their clients a real and meaningful service.

For the antitrust lawyer, there are two great rewards in practicing antitrust law. The first is that it is rarely boring. Almost every new client offers the opportunity to explore a new and different business and industry. Depending on its business, almost every new client's assignment offers a chance to see different parts of the economy and how they work. No two businesses are the same and no two industries work the same way. For the antitrust lawyer, it is challenging and occasionally fascinating to try to figure out how an industry works and why it works in one way as opposed to another.

The antitrust lawyer's second reward is that antitrust matters. At the end of the day, our free market economy works the way it does in great part because the fundamental rules for that economy are set in the antitrust laws. Few other lawyers can say that their daily work involves interpreting and applying our "the Magna Carta of free enterprise."

When You Need an Antitrust Lawyer

There are times when it will be obvious that antitrust counsel should be retained. Receipt of an antitrust grand jury subpoena, Department of Justice civil subpoena, or a plaintiff's antitrust complaint quickly come to mind. However, there are many instances where retaining antitrust counsel is prudent, but not obvious. Early identification of these situations and prompt retention of counsel is often critically important because antitrust counsel is frequently able to practice "preventive antitrust law" the way many doctors practice "preventive medicine." In other words, early involvement of antitrust counsel can often permit a business to avoid antitrust issues before taking action that converts those issues into antitrust investigations, lawsuits and the like. In short, in antitrust, as in medicine, an ounce of prevention can truly be worth a pound of cure.

A short, non-exhaustive list of situations in which antitrust counsel should be consulted follows:

Activities with competitors – Any activity in which the business interacts or cooperates with its competitors will likely be antitrust-sensitive. The heart of antitrust enforcement is stopping and preventing collusion among competitors. Such activity – price-fixing, bid-rigging and market allocation – is frequently prosecuted criminally. Not surprisingly, government antitrust enforcers are deeply suspicious of any joint activity by competitors. Such activity is often the subject of government investigation, either civil or criminal. Accordingly, before any activity with competitors is undertaken, antitrust counsel should be consulted to determine if the contemplated activity is appropriate and, if so, how the competitor communications can be managed to avoid any improper activity or information exchange. Equally important, counsel need to be consulted on how to avoid even the *appearance* of such activity.

Joint Ventures – Joint ventures with other firms, especially if they involve competitors, frequently raise antitrust questions that may make operation of the joint venture difficult or impossible. Antitrust counsel can frequently identify those issues (and hopefully offer solutions) before a significant investment of executive time is made in developing and negotiating the terms of the venture. Once the venture is established, antitrust counsel may need to monitor or police its operation to ensure that the venture does not become a vehicle for collusion among the parties in their competitive activities outside the venture.

Merger and Acquisitions – Significant corporate transactions frequently require merger clearances in the U.S., the European Union and other countries before they can be consummated. In addition, documents prepared or used by the parties in the transaction that analyze its competitive implications may have to be turned over to the Department of Justice and Federal Trade Commission as part of a Hart-Scott-Rodino premerger filing. Antitrust counsel should be contacted promptly when such transactions are contemplated, especially when competitors are involved. The early involvement of counsel may permit the parties to identify and address antitrust issues that may delay or derail the transaction. Counsel will also be able to help the parties develop a strategy for defending the deal and responding to any anticipated government investigation of the transaction.

Licenses – Restrictions imposed in connection with the licensing of trademarks, patents and copyrights frequently raise significant antitrust questions. Licensors often wish to include in their agreements limitations on licensees' prices and quantities, territories and customers to whom the business may sell, exclusivity provisions, and the like. Similarly, clients may wish to pool their Intellectual Property Rights with the similar rights of other licensors.

Distribution Questions – Any firm that is in the business of producing and/or selling goods or services through third parties will eventually encounter antitrust issues. Commonly encountered antitrust situations arise from, resale restrictions that the supplier wants to impose on its resellers, efforts to influence the price at which the resellers offer the supplier's product, changing a distribution strategy, terminating distributors or dealers, cooperative advertising plans and related promotional plans. All of these situations require guidance of antitrust counsel.

Working with Clients

As is true in most other areas of legal practice, clients who need antitrust counsel come in many different shapes and sizes and bring with them a wide variety of legal needs. Antitrust clients can range from individuals who are the victims of a price-fixing conspiracy, to small businesses that have disputes with their suppliers, to mid-size businesses trying to do a joint venture, to large multi-national companies facing a gamut of antitrust issues in their daily operations. Each of these clients has unique needs that require customized attention from counsel to ensure that the client's special concerns and problems are appropriately addressed.

In this connection is it is important to understand that some clients are extraordinarily sophisticated in terms of antitrust while others have little understanding or appreciation for the code of conduct the antitrust laws embody. Some business people instinctively understand antitrust or have been through investigations or large transactions before. As a result of that experience, they may have developed a good ear for knowing what is antitrust-sensitive and what is not. Others either have not had that experience or just do not have the gut sensitivity as to what works and what does not from the standpoint of antitrust compliance.

In addition, irrespective of a client's degree of sophistication, it will frequently be surprised by certain characteristics of government antitrust proceedings. For example, in an investigation, clients are almost uniformly surprised at the scope and intensity of the documentation the government wants. Responding to a government CID (Civil Investigative Demand), a grand jury subpoena or a Second Request for Information as part of a Hart-Scott-Rodino[43] merger review can be very burdensome and, in the eyes of many businessmen, astoundingly invasive. Responding to such information requests often imposes a real burden on the company. It takes a long time, is very expensive, and requires the attention of many people and often diverts management's attention from running the business. Perhaps more disturbing to the client, however, is the fact that such investigations require the disclosure of documents, e-mails and other communications that the client views as private to the business or personal to its employees. These concerns often become especially intense when it comes to the executives' own files that must be searched and perhaps produced in response to the government discovery demand.

Given the broad spectrum of clients, their relative degrees of sophistication and the antitrust issues they may face, antitrust counsel must deal with the client's needs in a nimble and flexible fashion. Responding to those needs precludes a "one size fits all" approach. For sophisticated clients with meaningful antitrust experience and real in-house antitrust knowledge and sensitivity, antitrust counsel needs to give refined, targeted, rifle shot counseling and representation. For less sophisticated clients, the representation may need to be far more hands-on with more fundamental advice and representation. It may also require doing things for the client that other clients may be able to do for themselves.

---

[43] Hart-Scott-Rodino Antitrust Improvements Act of 1976, 15 U.S.C. § 18a.

In the context of joint ventures, my sense is that, depending on the venture, management is usually surprised at how much time the venture takes, not only to put together, but to operate and police, as well. I suspect that financial surprises are not uncommon, that the expense of putting it together is always greater than expected, and that the time it takes to see if the venture succeeds is longer than expected – and frequently ventures fail. I think ventures fail especially when you are trying to create a new product; failure is part of the nature of new product development. And when you are trying to create a new product with somebody else, you have the added complexity of trying to coordinate.

Selected Antitrust Situations

Responding to Government Investigations
Perhaps the most stressful antitrust event a client will experience is the receipt of an antitrust grand jury subpoena, Department of Justice Civil Investigative Demand or Federal Trade Commission subpoena. Receipt of such documents frequently marks the beginning of a criminal or civil antitrust investigation of the company, its employees, its competitors or its entire industry. Such investigations are material events in the life of the client and must be treated with great care. In the most severe cases, criminal antitrust proceedings can result in jail sentences for the individuals involved, massive fines for the corporation and potentially enormous treble damage exposure to private plaintiffs. While civil investigations do not carry the risk of criminal prosecution and penalties,

they do carry their own risk of fines and frequently massive treble damage suits.[44]

A few examples should suffice to underscore the seriousness of such investigations and their aftermath. In the recent criminal charges brought in connection with the conspiracy between Christie's and Sotheby's, the world famous auctioneers of fine art, A. Alfred Taubman, the elderly former chairman of Sotheby's, was convicted of conspiring to fix prices and was sentenced to one year in prison plus $7.5 million in fines.[45] In addition, Sotheby's was forced to pay over $250 million in cash and other consideration to settle treble damage class action lawsuits.[46]

In a non-criminal proceeding, Mylan Laboratories, one of the world's leading manufacturers of generic drugs, was forced to disgorge $100 million to the Federal Trade Commission to settle charges that it had cornered the market for ingredients of certain popular medications and raised their prices several thousand percent.[47] In addition, Mylan was compelled to pay at least $35 million to settle private antitrust class actions.[48] In another case, the leading brokerage firms on Wall Street paid more than $1 billion to settle private treble damage claims that they fixed prices for trading on the NASDAQ stock market.[49]

---

44 Under the Clayton Act, antitrust violators may be sued by persons (individuals or businesses) injured by the violation for triple (treble) damages plus attorneys fees. 15 U.S.C. § 15.

45 See *United States v. A. Alfred Taubman*, Cr. No. 01 CR 429 (S.D.N.Y. 2001), *aff'd*, 297 F.3d 161 (2d Cir. 2002).

46 See *In re Auction Houses Antitrust Litigation*, 2001 WL 170792, *1 (S.D.N.Y. 2001).

47 *See* Statement of Chairman Robert Pitofsky, et al., *available at* http://www.ftc.gov/os/2000/11/mylanpitofskystatment.htm

48 *See* http://www.pomerantzlaw.com/publications/firmnewsUser2.cfm?pubid=290

49 *In re NASDAQ Market-Makers Antitrust Litigation*, 187 F.R.D. 465, 470 (S.D.N.Y. 1998).

Given the serious, potentially bankrupting repercussions of an investigation and resulting government enforcement proceeding, it is critical once the investigation begins for the client and counsel to determine as quickly as possible what potential violation the government is investigating, who it is investigating, whether the client is a target or subject of that investigation, and the degree of the client's involvement and exposure. This information will drive counsel's recommendations to the client and the strategy that will ultimately be pursued in addressing both the government's investigation and the likely (if not inevitable) private treble damage actions that will follow.

In responding to the investigation, perhaps the biggest and most important hurdle for the client and his counsel to clear is convincing the government attorneys handling the investigation that the client's involvement in the conduct under investigation was proper and legitimate. This is especially important (and potentially difficult) where the activity being investigated involves joint activity among competitors. Since such activity can result in price-fixing, market allocation and bid-rigging, the most serious antitrust offenses, the investigating agencies will be highly suspicious about the purpose and propriety of the competitors' communications and activities. The success or failure of the client and his counsel in persuading the investigating agency that the client's conduct was proper will likely determine the outcome of the investigation. That, in turn, will heavily influence any fines the client must pay and its degree of exposure in any subsequent treble damage litigation.[50]

---

50 Guilty pleas to criminal antitrust charges, convictions on such charges after trial or a judgment in favor of the government in a civil antitrust case can be used by a private plaintiff to establish that it has a prima facie case against the defendant in its subsequent civil case seeking treble damages. 15 U.S.C. § 16(a). It is therefore hardly surprising that the price of settling a treble damage case will

Joint Ventures

Joint ventures can offer businesses substantial economic benefits and cost savings and are actually encouraged by the federal government.[51] However, they can also raise significant antitrust concerns and, while rarely attacked, are often investigated by the Department of Justice or the Federal Trade Commission.

Joint ventures can be used for a wide variety of commercially useful purposes. They can be used to share the research and development costs (and risks) needed to develop a new product such as a new pharmaceutical or other technical product. They can be used by small firms to form joint purchasing groups that will enable each participant to obtain volume discounts from suppliers that the individual firms might not have sufficient volume to obtain separately. Joint ventures can also be used to share and reduce costs of critical but expensive facilities such as warehouses and transportation equipment. Finally, joint ventures can be used to create new products that no single competitor could create itself.[52]

While the joint ventures described above can all be perfectly lawful, potentially significant antitrust issues can arise when they involve competitors. The reason is obvious – participation in the venture may require cooperation and collaboration by the competitors and will certainly require communication between them. These communications may or may not be appropriate. In addition, the venture itself may

---

go up if the client has been charged by the government with an antitrust violation and has then pleaded guilty or been convicted after trial.

[51] *See* National Cooperative Research and Production Act of 1993, 15 U.S.C. §§ 4301-4305.

[52] For example, networks of Automated Teller Machines (ATMs) that make it possible to obtain cash from any bank's ATM, even by those who are not customers of that particular bank, are made possible by a joint venture among the banks who agree to participate in the ATM network.

eliminate competition among the competing partners in the venture, raising potentially serious antitrust concerns.[53]

For example, if competitors form a joint venture to develop a new type of product that they could not realistically be expected to develop separately, that venture would likely be found to be lawful if investigated.[54] However, if as part of the venture the participants agree that they will all charge the same price for the new product, that agreement will render the venture (or at least the pricing agreement) unlawful.[55] Similarly, if the joint venture partners enter into a price-fixing or market allocation agreement and try to shield it from antitrust attack by calling it a joint venture, the government enforcement agencies will disregard the joint venture label and attack the agreement as a *per se* illegal "naked restraint" of trade.[56]

Given the tension between the pro-competitive aspects of joint ventures and the anti-competitive aspects that can emerge, it is important that businesses embarking on joint ventures be able to identify efficiencies the venture will create. The client and his counsel must be able to demonstrate that the parties to the venture are all making real contributions to the venture and that efficiencies in the form of new products, cost savings or the ability to extend the parties' competitive reach will result. This is important because such contributions and savings are a significant marker the government will look at in determining whether the venture is real and has a legitimate business

---

[53] Federal Trade Comm'n & U.S. Dep't of Justice, *Antitrust Guildelines for Collaborations Among Competitors*, April 2000, at § 3.31(a) (hereinafter, *JV Guidelines*).
[54] *JV Guidelines*, § 3.3.
[55] *JV Guidelines*, § 3.2.
[56] *Id.*

purpose.[57] Assuming it does, and assuming the venture is what the government calls a "genuine integration of assets," where two or more entities are making real contributions of assets, talent, money and time to create something new or to generate true savings, the enforcement agencies will likely conclude that the venture is legitimate.[58]

Once the enforcement agencies determine that the venture is genuine and is not a facade for an otherwise illegal agreement among competitors, it will evaluate the venture to determine if there are "collateral restrictions" imposed on the venture or its participants that are themselves anti-competitive.[59] Such restrictions could take the form of agreements not to develop products that compete with the joint venture product or to deal exclusively with the venture. Such agreements may raise competition concerns depending on the facts specific to the venture and its participants. The agencies will also look to see if the venture itself has effects on competition, sometimes called spillover effects, that may be anti-competitive.[60] Both of these issues will be included in any antitrust review of the venture.

Given the potential sensitivity of joint ventures, especially those involving competitors, a thorough antitrust review of the venture should be done before the client makes any significant investment of time and resources into negotiating the terms of the venture with the other venture participants. The first questions that should be answered during the antitrust review are: What is the business reason for entering into the venture? What does the client expect to gain from it? Why can't the client achieve the same result on its own? Will the joint venture affect the client's relationships with its competitors in their activities outside

---

[57] JV Guidelines, § 3.36.
[58] JV Guidelines, § 3.2.
[59] JV Guidelines, §3.31(b).
[60] JV Guidelines,§3.32.

the venture? If so, how? Will the venture affect the nature of competition between the client and its competitors who are not included in the venture? Will anyone (either customers, suppliers or other competitors) be injured by the venture? If so, who will be hurt and how? Answers to these questions may be critically important in determining if the venture raises antitrust questions and, if so, whether those questions should be cause for concern.

Mergers and Acquisitions – Due Diligence

Mergers and Acquisitions constitute an area of antitrust practice unto itself. Entire books have been devoted to the subject and it would not be appropriate here to summarize the antitrust law of mergers and acquisitions. The kind of merger analysis done in the United States and in Europe, the kind of pre-merger filing regimes that different countries have and how all of it differs can provide endless grist for discussions among antitrust lawyers but is not especially useful for business executives. It is enough for businessmen to know that their mergers and acquisitions may require pre or post merger filings in many countries in addition to the United States and that the substantive merger review approaches used by different jurisdictions, notably the United States and the European Commission, may lead to different results.[61]

What businessmen should know about, however, are the antitrust risks that can arise during the due diligence process in transactions between competitors. Due diligence in mergers and acquisitions frequently occurs before antitrust lawyers are brought into the picture and, consequently, the parties to the transaction may not be sensitive to antitrust issues that due diligence can raise. In addition, since business executives will likely

---

[61] The best known example is the now abandoned merger between General Electric and Honeywell which was approved by U.S. antitrust regulators and blocked by the competition authorities in the EU.

have dozens of other issues to contend with during the merger negotiation process, the antitrust significance of due diligence is not likely to be considered. It is for that reason that the issue is addressed here.

During the due diligence process, merging parties disclose to each other massive amounts of confidential information about their respective businesses. Such disclosure should not be surprising. Before two parties commit millions or billions of dollars to a transaction, they must be certain that the business they seek to combine with is what it appears to be. The responsibilities that each firm's senior management owes to its board of directors and shareholders demand nothing less. However, where the merging firms are competitors, due diligence may include the disclosure of information concerning pricing, marketing plans, strategic plans, new product initiatives and the like. Such information, which goes to the heart of the rivalry between the two firms, would ordinarily be viewed by each firm as highly confidential and would never be disclosed to the other.

From an antitrust standpoint, the parties' reluctance to share highly confidential competitive information with a competing firm is a good thing. Sharing such information is frequently the first step toward a price-fixing agreement or other agreement eliminating competition between rivals. Indeed, in at least one case, the Federal Trade Commission brought an administrative proceeding against two merging parties who exchanged product-specific price information during due diligence.[62] In order to close the deal, however, it may be necessary to share at least some highly sensitive competitive data.

---

[62] See *In re Insilco Corp.*, FTC Docket No. C-3783 (1998).

There are usually ways to complete due diligence between merging firms in an antitrust appropriate manner. Antitrust lawyers have developed a number of approaches over the years to permit the parties to see the data they need without raising antitrust concerns. However, once the parties have shared sensitive information without using the protective measures developed by counsel, there may be little that can be done to correct the situation. Accordingly, before due diligence proceeds with respect to competitively sensitive information, antitrust counsel should be consulted.

Future Trends – the Internationalization of Antitrust Law

There have been many changes in antitrust law over the last decade. Many of those changes will continue and will likely affect businesses that come into contact with the antitrust authorities. Perhaps the most significant trend is the internationalization of antitrust. Nearly one hundred countries now have antitrust regimes and scores have some sort of merger filing requirements similar to our Hart-Scott-Rodino rules. That degree of merger control did not exist in any meaningful way fifteen years ago outside of the European Union, a couple of Western European countries, Canada, and the United States.

Now, when a client does a transaction, even if it appears to be entirely a domestic U.S. transaction, consideration must be given to the potential need to obtain merger clearance in the European Union, specific European countries, South America, Eastern Europe, Asia, and Africa.

In addition to different procedural merger clearance regimes, the different competition agencies frequently apply different substantive tests in their merger reviews. This, along with the fact that the markets and competitive realities may differ between countries, may lead to different results by different merger control authorities over the same merger. The best known example of this phenomenon is the GE-Honeywell merger which was cleared in the U.S., but blocked by the European Commission.

The complexity of obtaining multiple merger clearances under different merger review regimes, in countries with different merger review standards, converts the merger review process for cross-border transactions into a game of three-dimensional chess. This trend, which will likely continue, puts a serious burden, in terms of both time and resources, on parties trying to complete transactions. At some point there will be great pressure put on the merger control agencies to coordinate and unify at least some parts of their merger regimes. This may become a significant trend in the future.

Beyond the merger front, the internationalization of antitrust has other ramifications for the operations of international businesses. Many firms are learning, for example, that practices that are lawful in the U.S. may not be so in the EU. This applies to distribution restraints and intellectual property licensing. As a result, a client may find that key elements of its business model, which are lawful in the U.S., are not in various foreign countries. This may require a client to make significant changes to its business approach on a country-by-country basis. As the world economy becomes more globalized, it can be expected that these national differences in antitrust law will become an increasing burden on business.

Conclusion

For the business executive, antitrust is a fact of life. For growing businesses, it may become an increasingly important element in their ongoing operations. Executives of such firms would be well advised to consult with their antitrust counsel early and often to take full advantage of the benefits antitrust law offers them and to avoid the serious repercussions that can result from their violation.

James J. Calder devotes his practice to antitrust and antitrust litigation.

Mr. Calder's antitrust practice includes litigation, counseling and responding to Government antitrust investigations. He has handled matters involving price-fixing, market allocation, group boycotts and other horizontal restraints, monopolization, intellectual property licensing and other intellectual property issues, industry-wide standard setting efforts, vertical restraints, distribution issues and Robinson-Patman Act problems.

Mr. Calder also represents parties to U.S. and cross-border mergers and acquisitions. His M&A work includes substantive antitrust merger analysis, Hart-Scott-Rodino and foreign merger clearance compliance, responding to U.S. and foreign Government merger investigations and negotiating or litigating resolutions in contested merger situations. He also provides antitrust representation in the structuring and operation of domestic and international joint ventures and other collaborative efforts among competitors.

Mr. Calder's litigation practice includes antitrust, competitive tort, commercial and reinsurance cases and arbitrations. Mr. Calder also represents market makers on the NASDAQ in SEC and NASD enforcement matters.

A member of the Antitrust Section of the American Bar Association, Mr. Calder has served as Vice Chair of its Civil Practice & Procedure Committee. He was a member of the ABA's Antitrust Section Task Force that reviewed proposed legislation to repeal or modify the Supreme Court's decision in Illinois Brick Co. v. Illinois, as well as the Antitrust Section Task Force that drafted Sample Jury Instructions in Civil Antitrust Cases. Mr. Calder is also a member of the Antitrust and Trade Regulation Committee of the Association of the Bar of the City of New York.

Mr. Calder is a member of the New York Bar and is admitted to practice before the U.S. District Courts for the Southern and Eastern Districts of New York, the U.S. Courts of Appeals for the Second and Third Circuits and the U.S. Supreme Court. Mr. Calder received his undergraduate degree, with high distinction, from the University of Virginia (B.A., 1974), where he was a member of Phi Beta Kappa. He received his law degree from the University of Virginia Law School (J.D., 1977), where he was a Hardy Dillard fellow.

Acknowledgement –

The author gratefully acknowledges the assistance of Richard S. Julie, an associate at Katten Muchin Zavis Rosenman, in the preparation of this article.

The Foundation of Antitrust Law

Lewis A. Noonberg

Partner
Piper Rudnick LLP

Understanding the Antitrust Laws

Early Trends

Understanding the antitrust laws today and making some reasonable predictions about their future require three things: One, some knowledge of the purposes of the antitrust laws as expressed in Congressional debates 113 years ago; two, some knowledge of how courts have interpreted the sweeping language of Section 1 of the Sherman Act as well as other statutory provisions over the last 35 years; and three, some "chutzpah."[63]

The original purposes of the antitrust laws enacted in 1890 were to (a) break up the "trusts" that had evolved by the late 1800s (like the Oil Trust and the Sugar Trust) which were controlling large segments of industry; (b) protect small business against the perceived ravages of the owners of these trusts; and (c) protect the consumer. In 1890, no one considered that there might be inconsistencies in promoting these three goals. Moreover, economic power resided "upstream" in 1890. There were no Wal Marts at the turn of the 19th century – not even any A&Ps – so the effort was to curb the power of manufacturers and to protect those businesses downstream, i.e., wholesalers and retailers. It was assumed that what was good for wholesalers and retailers was also good for the consumer. Perhaps the epitome of this assumption is found in the Supreme Court's *Schwinn* decision (388 U.S. 365 (1967)) holding that once a manufacturer conveyed title and dominion over a product, it was a *per se* violation of the antitrust laws to restrict the purchaser's ability to resell it by restricting who the purchaser could resell to, where the purchaser could resell it, or the price at which the product could be resold.

---

[63] Commonly-used Yiddish word meaning something like "foolishly fearless."

However, shortly thereafter, economic and academic writings severely criticized these rules as protecting the status quo and actually harming the consumer. In the seminal work by Judge Robert Bork, entitled "The Antitrust Paradox", published in 1978, he persuasively argued that prohibition of these types of vertical restraints (i.e. restraint by seller on its purchaser's right to resell) were standing the antitrust laws on their head, and ignoring the fact that real competition did not exist between a buyer and a seller (a vertical relationship), but rather between two sellers or even between two buyers (a horizontal relationship) and restraints on resales imposed by a manufacturer on its wholesale or retail dealer might actually enhance competition between two different manufacturers of the same type of product (referred to as *inter*brand competition, as opposed to *intra*brand competition, which is competition between or among sellers of the same product.) The Supreme Court recognized this explicitly in the *Continental TV* case in 1977 (433 U.S. 36) going out of its way to overrule *Schwinn*. In *Continental TV*, the court held that non-price vertical restraints imposed by a manufacturer on its dealers were not *per se* illegal. (Subsequent cases have recognized that absent monopoly power in the seller, non-price vertical restraints were unlikely to violate the antitrust laws, *per se* or not.) Despite the logical inconsistencies, price related vertical restraints remained *per se* violations.[64]

The Rise of the Chicago School of Economics

This set the stage for the most significant sea change in antitrust enforcement in 90 years, i.e. the rise of "The Chicago School of Economics" or "Reagonomics," which got into full swing in 1981 when

---

[64] Subsequently, in State v. Oil Co. v. Kahn, 118 S.Ct. 275 (1997), the Supreme Court held that price related vertical restraints that put a cap on the maximum amount a purchaser could charge in the resale transaction were not per se violations, and might even be pro-consumer.

President Reagan appointed Professor William Baxter as Assistant Attorney General in charge of the Antitrust Division of the Department of Justice. Professor Baxter, formerly with Stanford University, implemented Chicago School economics into antitrust enforcement. At the risk of oversimplifying his views, he believed: (a) All vertical arrangements or restrictions (price and non-price) were competitively neutral. The issue was whether there was collusive activity between or among competing sellers. Using an example he would ask, why would Ford Motor Company restrict its Ford dealers in how they could resell Ford automobiles? Not to harm its own dealers, and certainly not to impede consumers from purchasing Ford automobiles, but rather to set up a distribution system that was more effective in selling cars against its real competitor, Chevrolet (interbrand competition), even if it meant putting restraints on how or where or to whom Ford dealers could sell Ford automobiles, thus restricting competition between one Ford dealer and another –intrabrand competition; (b) He also believed that the manufacturer, with its huge investment in plant and machinery, had a greater incentive in moving product through the distribution process faster and cheaper than a wholesaler or retailer who might be selling many different products and who might want to sell fewer products of a particular manufacturer, but at a higher price. Thus, the third element – and perhaps the most controversial – that the manufacturer was significantly more of a surrogate for the consumer than those wholesalers or retailers downstream; (c) Manufacturers should not have to face an antitrust jury every time they wanted to change distributors. Thus, the Supreme Court in *Monsanto Co. v. Spray-Rite Serv. Corp.*, 465 U.S. 752 (1984) and in the *Business Electronics* case, 485 U.S. 717 (1988), made it significantly harder for terminated dealers and distributors to get to a jury in an antitrust case following termination by a manufacturer. The result, from the manufacturer's point of view, has been to allow faster, cheaper, changes in their distribution policies. From the dealer or distributor's point of view, the change has been to make these downstream entities subservient to their manufacturers.[65] On this issue, the academic debate continues, and the courts have more recently backed off pure Chicago School analysis. In the *Eastman Kodak* case, 504 U.S. 451 (1992), the Supreme Court specifically recognized that markets do not always work the way economists expect them to, and competition downstream (among retailers, even retailers selling the same product) may be as important as competition upstream (among separate manufacturers). Thus, today, antitrust jurisprudence resides somewhere between these two versions of antitrust jurisprudence.

The Robinson-Patman Paradox

Two additional macro trends in antitrust law need to be considered. First, in 1936, at a time many consider to be one of the worst years of The Great Depression, Congress passed what is known as the Robinson-Patman Price Discrimination Law ("R-P Act"). Although enacted as part and parcel of the package of federal antitrust laws, the R-P Act had, as a stated goal price, uniformity. On its surface, the R-P Act made eminent good sense – with certain exceptions, all buyers from a single manufacturer should pay the same price for the goods they bought. One of the stated purposes of the R-P Act is to protect "Ma & Pa" retailers (particularly local food markets) from the ravages of the chain store's buying power, and particularly the ravages of what was then considered the most rapacious chain store, A&P. The difficulties, however, were (a) that price uniformity is inconsistent with the Sherman Act's price flexibility goals which are designed to encourage reduced prices; and (b)

---

[65]   In certain industries, such as gasoline service stations and automobile dealerships, Congress passed special statutes limiting the power of manufacturers to control their dealers. See Petroleum Marketing Practices Act, 15 USCA §§ 2801-2841, and the Automobile Dealers' Day in Court Act, 15 USCA §§ 1221-1225.

the R-P Act is a model of poor draftsmanship.[66] As a result, R-P Act enforcement has been sporadic at best.

New Areas of Antitrust Enforcement

The second macro trend has been enforcement of the Sherman Act in fields where it had been thought to be inapplicable. In the 1970's, antitrust enforcement came to the real estate industry, particularly shopping center development. No discount clauses, veto clauses, radius clauses, and exclusives came under attack by the FTC despite the perception up to that time that real estate development was local and therefore did not implicate the antitrust laws. In the 1980's, health care providers including hospitals, doctor groups and third-party payers came under attack in peer review situations, tie-ins and mergers despite the fact that up until the late 1970's, the perception was that the antitrust laws were not applicable to the professions, i.e. the professions were not involved in "trade or commerce" as defined by the antitrust laws. In the 1990's, the antitrust laws focused their attention on the securities industry with attacks on various industry practices which were said to amount to price fixing despite the perception up to that time that the securities industry was exempt from antitrust scrutiny principally because of the industry's comprehensive regulation by the SEC.

In the healthcare field, there is a triumvirate, the members of which are generally at odds with one another. There is the institutional provider, the hospital; there is the third-party payer, the HMO or the insurance

---

[66]   A discussion describing the examples of poor draftsmanship of the R-P Act is beyond the scope of this paper. Suffice it to say, both the defenders of the R-P Act as well as its detractors agree that the Act is internally inconsistent.

company; and then there are the doctors and doctor groups, to say nothing of the consumer who gets tossed around in all of this.

What has happened is that economic power has shifted from individual healthcare providers (the doctors) to the third-party payers for a number of reasons including supply/demand shifts, Congressional incentives to reduce hospital stays and because the Supreme Court and other courts have said: The third-party payer is the surrogate for the consumer. As a "group buyer," it has the ability to create downward pressure on prices; whereas, doctors, who are independent sellers of services, cannot band together in order to push back against that power unless they are true partners – and doctors are famous for not wanting to form big partnerships. They have felt the impact of this downward pressure on prices, along with increased costs, particularly malpractice insurance. This broad, sweeping shift in economic power from sellers of healthcare services to buyers of healthcare services, or, more accurately, their surrogates, the third-party payers is the most significant and dramatic shift in economic power I have ever seen.

There are bills now pending in Congress and in various state legislatures to allow doctors to engage in collective bargaining with third-party payers even though they are separate economic entities, but no significant legislation has passed to date, despite great pressure from the American Medical Association. Of course, competition has also come to the institutional provider – the hospitals, as they face competitive challenges. If you doubt it, ask yourself why hospitals are advertising, merging and developing specialized niches.

As noted above, the antitrust laws have also focused on the securities industry, beginning in 1994, when two previously not very well known finance professors wrote an article that asked why quotes on the NASDAQ stocks were always in even eighths, never in odd eighths, meaning the figures were ¼, ½, and ¾, or the whole number, never 3/8, 5/8 or 7/8. As a result, the SEC, the NASD, the Department of Justice, and class action private treble damage suits were brought virtually the next day. That began a whole series of matters wherein plaintiffs' lawyers, the DOJ, and the SEC, in addition to the SEC's concern about violations of SEC rules, asserted that these activities were coordinated anticompetitive actions among competitors. A number of these cases are still pending. And so today, we have antitrust coverage in all these areas that were not too long ago considered outside the domain of antitrust enforcement.

The Clayton Act Anti-Merger Provisions

Finally, a broad review of 113 years of antitrust jurisprudence would not be complete without a brief discussion of what became Section 7 of the Clayton Act (adopted in 1914), 15 U.S.C.A. § 18, the Anti-Merger provision. While trends in antitrust enforcement of § 7 have evolved along with trends in industrial organization economics, the principal focus has been on its prophylactic purpose. Section 7 authorizes attacks on mergers (principally mergers of competitors) which are "likely" to have an adverse effect on competition. A full-blown anticompetitive effect need not be demonstrated. The focus is on the relevant product and geographic market. The Court asks, is the likely effect of the merger anticompetitive in some product line in some area of the country? To determine whether it is likely to be anticompetitive, courts (or the FTC or the Antitrust Division of the Department of Justice) ask: Will the combined company be able to raise prices for their combined products above existing competitive prices or will they, as a combined power, be able to exclude other competitors from the market for those products. An affirmative answer to either question is likely to result in a challenge to the merger. Obviously, a determination of the scope of the relevant market and the likelihood of an adverse effect are issues that require economic, legal, and sometimes marketing expertise because courts want to know what the effects are on the purchasers of the goods or services sold by the combined entity.

Monopolization and Other Issues

While the antitrust laws cover a myriad of other issues such as monopolization, attempted monopolization and conspiracy to monopolize (§ 2 of the Sherman Act, 15 U.S.C.A. § 2) and tie-ins and exclusive dealing agreements (§ 3 of the Clayton Act, 15 U.S.C.A. 3), those issues historically have generally not been in the forefront of antitrust law jurisprudence, although very recent cases (*U.S. v. Microsoft*, 253 F.3d 34 (D.C. Cir. 2001); *LePage's v. 3M*, 2003 WL1480498 (3rd Cir. 2003), and *Conwood Company v. U.S. Tobacco*, 2002 Fed. App. 0171 (6th Cir. 2002), along with *Coca Cola v. Harmar Bottling Co.*, a Texas Court of Appeals case (85 ATRR 2116), decided July 17, 2003, all upholding monopolization claims, may signal increased § 2 monopolization enforcement.

Turning from the macro to the micro, a few specifics about § 1 seem appropriate, since it is perhaps the fundamental building block for all antitrust jurisprudence (with the exception of the R-P Act).

Some "Micro" Points About § 1 of the Sherman Act

Section 1 of the Sherman Act: Per se violations
Agreements among sellers to fix, stabilize, or maintain prices;

Agreements among sellers to allocate markets, such as two competitors agreeing "you sell to this group of buyers, and I'll sell to another group and we will not compete with each other";

Joint boycotts, i.e., two competitors agreeing not to sell to or buy from a particular third party.

These types of agreements carry with them the potential for a criminal felony conviction, although only price fixing and market-allocation actually result in criminal prosecution. It is always surprising to learn that otherwise sensible, sound, successful business people sometimes forget that these are potentially criminal activities.

For example, very recently a 78-year-old billionaire, who made his fortune in the shopping-center business, was convicted of price fixing in connection with his ownership of a major auction house in July 2002 and coordinating its commission practices with another major auction house.

There is a fourth activity known as tie-ins, about which courts are somewhat inconsistent. While tie-in agreements are usually regarded as *per se* violations, they require proof of an adverse effect in a market. Other *per se* violations do not require proof of an adverse market impact. Price fixing or market allocation agreements are conclusively presumed to have adversely affected the market, no proof of market impact (or lack thereof) is needed or relevant.

Some Personal Reflections about Effective Representation of Clients

Fundamental Role of the Antitrust Lawyer

Antitrust lawyers – *not* professors or judges – advise clients about potential activity and whether those activities might violate the antitrust laws. They help clients achieve legitimate business objectives in a way that avoids, not evades, antitrust liability.

Second, an antitrust lawyer's role is to defend a client who has been charged with a violation of the antitrust laws, whether it is by the government or in private litigation, to the extent consistent with the law, or to prosecute an antitrust violation as vigorously as the law allows.

Third, an antitrust law practitioner today can represent both plaintiffs and defendants. In some fields, for instance in labor relations law, a lawyer is usually on one side or another, labor or management. In the antitrust field, 20 years ago, major companies would never have thought of being plaintiffs in an antitrust case; and now they *do* exercise their rights to bring antitrust cases.

Area of Concentration

My own practice consists of representing businesses as a consultant or litigator or both, either in court or before federal or state agencies. The common theme is application of antitrust law principles.

It is also rewarding to concentrate on particular industries. Presently, the healthcare and securities industries, and to some extent, real estate-related matters have been my principal litigation and consulting focus, although in recent years, manufacturers and retailers as well as importers have been the focus of my antitrust work.

Make Friends, Cut Risks, Help Clients

Another issue is how to deal with public agencies. In my opinion, it is always a good idea to deal with them candidly and cooperatively. For the most part, they are good lawyers and economists. You and your client are making a big mistake if you try to keep your cards close to the vest and then slide something through. It is virtually always a mistake. If you have an issue, my view is to deal with it openly, and in that way the agencies, just like any other business, have a sense of trust in the lawyers with whom they are dealing.

The added value that a good antitrust lawyer brings to his or her client is not only knowing the law, but also knowing how markets work. The antitrust laws are not just torts – they deal with markets, and always ask the question, did some agreement (or merger) for the sale of goods or services harm a market?

Thus, antitrust lawyers make judgments about markets, who the players are, who competes with whom, where competition exists, and what the choices are that a consumer has. Dealing with those kinds of issues, in the context of what are the parameters of the market and what effect, if any, the activity in question is having in that market, is what antitrust lawyers do for a living.

So competition is not a mathematical certainty, and if you believe in mathematical certainty, you are not cut out to be an antitrust lawyer.

Strategies with Clients

When a client sits down with you and says, "I received a subpoena or a CID (civil investigative demand) from an agency questioning an agreement that I have made." The approach is, number one, to figure out what is bothering the agency about the program. And second, what is the real reason this agreement was entered into? By the way, this is a very simple question, but it very often leads to some very helpful or troubling information.

If, when you ask the reason for entering into this agreement, the answer comes back, "Well, if you want to know the truth, it's because we figured we could squeeze out our competitors," that tells you something. But if, on the other hand, the answer is, "Because we thought we could operate more efficiently," that also tells you something. If the client can't answer the question, you know there is some concern somewhere.

If you get the right answer to the first question, then one needs to figure out what impact it has, or why the FTC or the DOJ, or some attorney general in some state is concerned about it. At that point, you may or may not retain an economist to help you understand the economic impact. Keep in mind that the antitrust agencies, both the DOJ and FTC, have economists, as well as the lawyers, reviewing each deal, whether it is a competition complaint or a merger. Make certain you have somebody who is very skilled at understanding what the Bureau of Economics of the FTC is saying to its lawyers about this deal and how you should respond to it.

With respect to a proposed merger, you should assess whether you think it will be challenged and if so, why. Are there ways to fix the problem? Other considerations: Do you need to get an economist now? Is the merger likely to get the "infamous" Second Request? A Second Request is a questionnaire from the government asking more in-depth multi-part questions. You try to figure out whether that is coming and try to avoid it by answering questions ahead of time.

In terms of litigation, you try to figure out what has been done, what the client's objective is, and whether it is something that should be settled or something you have a chance of winning. Estimate the cost, and try to be candid about it and the exposures.

In some respects, the antitrust laws favor plaintiffs in litigation in significant ways. First of all, actual damages are automatically trebled, plus reasonable attorney's fees. Second, losing defendants have no right of indemnity or contribution among each other, and each is responsible for the entire amount. For example, if you have two defendants that engaged in price-fixing, and both are sued, and the plaintiff wins, the plaintiff can decide to collect the entire trebled amount from one defendant. The other defendant can't say, "We did this together," so we should share the liability.

This puts tremendous leverage in the hands of plaintiffs to obtain a settlement. That is what Congress wanted and why you see so many treble-damage class action antitrust cases settled. The deck is stacked, but again, that is what Congress wanted to do.

New Roles for Antitrust Laws

Intersection of Antitrust and the Intellectual Property Laws
Timothy J. Muris, Chairman of the FTC, pointed out recently that the intersection between the antitrust laws and what we can generally refer to as intellectual property protection is at the forefront of antitrust enforcement today.

The Hatch-Waxman Act was enacted by Congress to encourage the development of generic drugs to compete with the pioneer drugs. An unintended consequence of that Act is to provide incentives for pioneer drug companies to pay the generic to stay out of the market. These agreements are at the core of recent antitrust enforcement efforts.

Hospital Mergers Revisited
Second, again Chairman Muris's point – the FTC is going to take a retrospective look at hospital mergers that the FTC and DOJ have been relatively unsuccessful in stopping. Muris wants to see whether the results of those decisions have been anticompetitive. Although it may be difficult, the government is never stopped from revisiting an

anticompetitive condition, particularly a newly created one originally opposed by the government.

The efforts to stop a merger before the merger occurs are prophylactic, and you have to make all kinds of econometric projections as to what is going to happen in the future. So now that all that has happened, Muris is saying, let's go back and see what really happened. The effect of these two enforcement efforts likely will shape antitrust laws in the future.

Lewis Noonberg's primary area of practice is in antitrust and commercial litigation and counseling, particularly in the financial services, health care, food processing, manufacturing and real estate industries. He has appeared as lead counsel in major antitrust cases in district courts and courts of appeal throughout the United States. He serves as national trade regulation counsel for several clients in various industries, as well as representing and counseling clients involved in federal and state antitrust investigations.

Mr. Noonberg has taught various courses at the Georgetown University Law Center and University of Maryland School of Law, including Antitrust Law and Antitrust and Health Care Law, and has lectured extensively in continuing professional education courses on antitrust law. He has also lectured at The Johns Hopkins University on business law.

Mr. Noonberg served as an assistant attorney general of Maryland for two years, representing various state agencies including the Maryland Insurance Division. He served as chair of Piper Rudnick's Antitrust & Trade Regulation practice group for over 15 years.

He received his LL.B. from the University of Maryland School of Law in 1962 and his A.B. from Dartmouth College in 1959.

The View of an Antitrust M&A Practitioner

Michael H. Byowitz

Partner, Head of Antitrust Department
Wachtell, Lipton, Rosen & Katz

The Goals of Antitrust

The antitrust laws of the United States are premised on the belief that competition in the marketplace maximizes consumer welfare. The antitrust laws are based on a philosophy that markets typically work, and that if left free of artificial restraints, competition assures that markets function to produce the optimal level of goods and services for consumers at the lowest possible price. Because market participants may have incentives to engage in activities or transactions that interfere with or reduce competition, the antitrust laws seek to prevent unreasonable restrictions on the marketplace that interfere with the competitive process.

The antitrust laws are consistent with a major international trend that has been gaining acceptance during the past 10 or 15 years - a substantial movement in the direction of free-market economies in most of the world. Today, the world's strong economies are countries that to varying degrees have opted for free markets as opposed to managed economies. This trend, which has brought increased prosperity to many societies (as well as dislocations from time to time), is very likely to continue. Any shift in a different direction would be a substantial net detriment to world prosperity.

Because the competitive process is important for markets to function properly and thereby maximize societal welfare, and in view of the incentives that market participants may have to try artificially to distort that process, the adoption of antitrust laws (frequently referred to outside the United States as competition laws) is seen as a vital component of the movement to market economies. As a result, numerous countries around the world have adopted competition laws in the past decade. At last count, there were well over 100 countries with at least some antitrust laws, including more than 70 countries that impose requirements for filing with a government antitrust authority prior to consummating mergers, acquisitions and some joint ventures.

The Basics of Practice

The role of the antitrust lawyer is to provide guidance to clients in an understandable and practical way as to the legal restrictions that the antitrust laws place on their conduct and the transactions in which they may engage. A good antitrust lawyer helps clients achieve their legitimate business objectives in ways that minimize legal risks and avoid the substantial penalties, proceedings, expenses, diversions and embarrassments that can result from violations of the antitrust laws.

It is important to approach antitrust cases with a substantial degree of common sense, and an ability to explain economic and legal concepts in pragmatic terms. Antitrust is fact intensive and strategies for dealing with an antitrust case or transaction vary considerably. The facts are key in many areas of law, but particularly in antitrust. The antitrust cases decided by the United States Supreme Court tend to involve an extensive review of the industry and the practices or transactions at issue. Every industry is different with discrete market participants, competitive dynamics, entry conditions and types and numbers of customers. The same approach is not necessarily appropriate in every transaction or activity.

This is particularly true in the area in which I work principally - corporate mergers, acquisitions and joint ventures. No two mergers are alike. A cookie-cutter approach will not be successful in dealing with transactions that are reviewed by the world's major competition law enforcement agencies such as the Federal Trade Commission ("FTC") and the Antitrust Division of the Department of Justice (the "DOJ") in the United

States, the Commission of the European Union (the "EU" or "European Commission") and various individual countries in Europe, and the Canadian Competition Bureau, among others.

In advising clients, generally I review the risks of contemplated conduct or transaction, and let the client decide whether it wants to take the risk or not, although I tell the client why I think running the risk would or would not be reasonable. Most antitrust advice involves rule of reason situations where if you fully understand what the client is trying to accomplish, you can advise the client that while there is a hypothetical risk, it is remote and a reasonable one to take given strong legitimate business reasons. However, that is certainly not the case with regard to cartel activities, which involve potentially enormous fines in many jurisdictions and criminal sanctions including serious jail time in the United States. In cartel situations, the only sensible advice is not to engage in the conduct.

Issues and Challenges

In representing clients in transactions, it is advisable at the outset to outline the process for reviewing transactions in the relevant jurisdiction(s) and ensure that the client has a good understanding of what is entailed in each stage of the process. Some corporations have had extensive experience with the antitrust merger review process in the United States and/or abroad while others (both large and small) have not. Even where the client is relatively sophisticated about the merger review process, an experienced and skilled antitrust lawyer will have greater knowledge of the legal requirements and the practical realities of the process. The client will have detailed knowledge of the industry and market participants. An effective antitrust lawyer will form a cooperative partnership with the client in which each brings something unique to the table. A good antitrust lawyer brings considerable experience with merger review in the United States to bear in a way that addresses the client's objectives in the merger, and elicits the industry facts and market-based arguments that may persuade an otherwise reluctant antitrust agency to let the transaction proceed. The client provides the factual basis from which those arguments can be formed.

To be more specific, the role of the antitrust lawyer in a merger involves multiple facets.

At the outset, antitrust counsel should advise a company whether and to what extent its potential merger is likely to be permitted or challenged by the relevant competition law authorities. This involves review of the industry and market facts (usually in an unavoidably short time and on the basis of information that is necessarily less than complete), and then providing an accurate prediction as to (1) whether the transaction can be consummated, (2) how long it is likely to take to complete the merger review process, and (3) whether and how much of the assets of the combined company are likely to have to be divested in order to complete the transaction.

Antitrust counsel should be involved in negotiating the antitrust risk allocation in the merger or asset purchase agreement. A seller wants to have reasonable assurance that the merger will be completed because its business may be damaged during the course of the investigation. A buyer doesn't want to commit to a level of divestitures that undercuts the synergies and strategic rationale for the merger. The sensitivities on each side vary depending on the particular circumstances of the parties in that some mergers are more likely to require higher levels of divestiture than others, some sellers have reason to want greater assurances of consummation than others, and the strategic imperatives of individual sellers differ. The right advice is necessary to assure that an agreement can be reached and each side is appropriately protected.

Antitrust counsel should advise companies throughout the merger review process on integration planning and avoiding concerns by the government agencies (particularly the FTC) about parties not engaging in what is referred to as "antitrust gun jumping." Mergers may ultimately succeed or fail as a business matter based on the level of advance planning that the acquirer can do, and it is very important to be able to "hit the ground running" once a merger is completed. Conversely, there is often a not inconsiderable possibility that the merger will not be completed for any number of reasons, so that the acquired company needs to preserve the confidentiality of its most sensitive business information until it is clear that the transaction will proceed. The diverging needs of the parties can normally be accommodated in ways that don't create legitimate concerns of enforcers concerning antitrust gun jumping, but this requires the ongoing involvement of the antitrust adviser.

Once the parties have entered into a binding agreement, antitrust counsel should work with the company and the other party's antitrust counsel to prepare the filing required under what is referred to in the US as the Hart-Scott-Rodino (HSR) Act and represent the company through the merger review process at the FTC/DOJ. It is also necessary to deal with any issues that may be raised by state attorneys general, who look at some mergers, usually in tandem with the federal antitrust authorities, and there may be a role to play with regard to any regulatory authorities that have concurrent jurisdiction (e.g., the Federal Communications Commission in telecommunication mergers).

While most mergers make it through the US review process without incident or at worst with some level of divestiture, there are a few each year that are challenged in court. If a merger is ultimately challenged by the FTC, DOJ, a state attorney general or a private party (private merger challenges are permitted in limited circumstances, and are rarely brought), antitrust counsel will work with litigators to defend the company and the merger.

Finally, from time to time some antitrust counsel represents companies in connection with hostile takeovers. In such transactions, antitrust counsel, whether representing the target or the raider, become involved in attempts by the target to persuade the government agencies (federal as well as state attorneys general) that the merger creates a competitive problem. There is also the possibility of the target bringing its own suit in federal court since targets have standing to bring such suits in certain federal appellate circuits.

Clients need to understand that even relatively small transactions are subject to review by the federal antitrust authorities in the United States under the HSR Act. Subject to certain recognized exemptions, a transaction whose value exceeds $50 million but is less than $200 million is typically reportable if it involves (1) a party with more than $100 million of total assets or sales and (2) the other party has more than $10 million in assets or sales. Transactions above $200 million generally are reportable without reference to the size of the transaction parties. If an HSR filing is required and the transaction raises potential competitive concerns, the client should be advised that completing the government review of the merger may entail a substantial amount of time and money. The agencies may learn of the competitive issues because they are revealed through the filing itself or when viewed together with other publicly available information. Even when that is not the case, the antitrust authorities may be prompted into investigating the transaction by complaints from interested third parties (*i.e.*, competitors, customers or suppliers).

To complete a reportable corporate merger or acquisition, the parties must file an HSR pre-merger notification and report form with the FTC and the DOJ. The filing triggers a mandatory waiting period of 30 days (15 days in cash tender offers). During the first waiting period, the FTC or DOJ may choose to conduct an initial review to determine whether the transaction appears to raise antitrust issues that merit a full investigation. If concerned about the merger's possible anti-competitive effects at the end of the initial waiting period, the reviewing agency will issue a request for additional information and documentary materials (a "Second Request"). The typical Second Request is an intensely burdensome set of document and information requests. The issuance of a Second Request causes a new waiting period of typically 30 days (10 days in cash tender offers) to commence, and this new waiting period does not begin to run until the parties have substantially complied with the Second Request. In many mergers, compliance with the Second Request can take months to complete, and in some very large transactions it has taken longer than a year. When dealing with a Second Request, the parties will normally have to copy prodigious amounts of documents and incur large expenses to search databases, computer systems, e-mail servers and the like. The only easy way around a Second Request is to convince the government, normally in the initial waiting period, that the transaction doesn't warrant a full investigation.

In addition to the burdens of a Second Request, the US merger review process frequently entails substantial time for employees to be interviewed or have their depositions taken by the reviewing agency. Many investigations cannot be completed successfully without extensive substantive submissions (referred to as white papers). It is frequently necessary to meet with the investigating staff, supervisory personnel and the head(s) of the agency – the Assistant Attorney General in charge of the Antitrust Division or the five Federal Trade Commissioners. In some cases, the process is prolonged by the need to negotiate a consent decree resolving certain antitrust concerns identified by the government. As a result, a full merger review is a time intensive process. You simply cannot convince one of the federal antitrust enforcement agencies to permit a transaction to proceed that appears to raise serious antitrust issues without a great deal of information and argument showing that there is not a competitive problem.

In effectively representing corporate clients in connection with the antitrust review of mergers and acquisitions, there are a number of strategies and methodologies that are useful to follow.

Learn the facts as rapidly and efficiently as you can.

Understand that the facts will come out. It is ineffective and counterproductive to make arguments that are not well grounded in the facts, so avoid them.

Work cooperatively with the reviewing agency to the maximum extent that is consistent with your client's interest.

Understand that adopting a confrontational approach with the government will cause them to play hardball, so don't do it except in very unusual cases.

Recognize that the government has interests that differ from your client's, and that some of the requests the government makes are not consistent with your client's interest. In such circumstances, either think of a way to avoid the problem or assert the client's interest vigorously but not in an unnecessarily confrontational way. Keep in mind that there are times where it is important to answer the questions asked without volunteering additional information. An antitrust lawyer must develop a well honed skill for knowing when that is appropriate and defensible conduct and when it is not.

The US agencies must go to court to stop mergers; they cannot block them on their own. Always be prepared to litigate the tough cases or at least let the government think that you are prepared to do so (again, this can be done in a non-confrontational way). The reviewing agency may hesitate to bring what it regards as a weak case or may be willing to accept a modest remedy that it wouldn't take in a stronger case.

Keep the client's objectives firmly in mind and be realistic about what you are trying to achieve during the course of the investigation. There are situations where it would be a great victory for the client to get the transaction through with a modest divestiture. In such a case, try to get the transaction completed with no divestment if that is in the client's interest, but not in a manner that may undercut the settlement that your client would be very pleased with at the end of the process. Remember that fighting on the merits in what is likely to be a lost cause may cause delay. This delay may impact the realization of synergies that may be of sufficient magnitude to outweigh the benefits that would come from avoiding all divestitures after the delay in obtaining these synergies is factored in. Advise the client of these countervailing considerations, and suggest the best way to address them.

There are two key factors that often dramatically impact the outcome of government investigations that may not be recognized initially by many clients.

First, what is said in party documents is critically important to whether a merger is challenged. This is particularly true as to what is said in so-called Item 4(c) documents. These are documents that discuss the merger. Specifically, Item 4(c) of the HSR Form requires the submission of:

All studies surveys, analyses and reports prepared by or for a director or officer of the filing company (or any of its subsidiaries) that analyze or evaluate the transaction in question with regard to competition, competitors markets, market shares, potential for sales growth or geographic market expansion.

These documents are submitted as part of the initial HSR filing, and they are looked at very carefully by reviewing staffs in the first waiting period. Item 4(c) documents can have a disproportionate effect on the outcome of an investigation; indeed, "bad" 4(c) documents may themselves trigger an investigation that might not otherwise occur. Only the final version or the last draft of each 4(c) document is called for by the Form. So it is very important for antitrust counsel to review potential 4(c) documents in draft form before they are finalized. Clients should be encouraged to take out or correct unhelpful and inaccurate statements that are made by merger advocates within a company. The agencies maintain that Item 4(c) covers offering memoranda and investment banker books even when the specific acquirer of the company or assets in question had not been determined when the document was prepared. Antitrust counsel should have an opportunity to provide comments on such materials as soon as possible.

Second, customer reaction matters considerably, and competitors can be an important source of information for the reviewing agency. When customers are unhappy about a merger, it is more likely that there will be a full investigation, significant divestitures will be required and the merger will be challenged by the agency or even blocked in court. In many mergers, customers and competitors are themselves sophisticated companies with their own antitrust lawyers who know how to make their views known to the government in an effective manner. In any event, the government is going to ask such third parties about basic industry facts that the client is asserting. If customers in particular disagree with the client's version of reality, it is going to be hard to convince the government; this is the case even if it is only a vocal minority of customers who are providing a different story. So if a merger appears to raise an antitrust issue, I advise the client to promote the merger to its customers from the outset and let those who express concern know why the merger is not a problem. This is good business practice in any event. A merger is a major event for customers, and each party has important business reasons to be reassuring customers that they should continue existing business relationships while a merger is pending.

I've been asked about the attributes essential to be a great antitrust lawyer. In mergers and acquisitions, there are several important ones that I have identified:

It is important to be able to reasonably predict what is likely to happen during the merger process, and to be able to work the process to achieve as good or better a result than the client might reasonably expect. This involves not only extensive experience but a great deal of common sense. Be objective. Don't be reluctant to tell the client things that the client may not be happy to hear (at least at first blush), if that is necessary to help the client understand and successfully negotiate the process. Be prepared to try to convince the client to pursue the course that you believe is most consistent with its interests.

At the same time, there are frequently very smart people at the client who know the industry much better than the lawyer ever will and also have their own business experiences that may be usefully applied to the merger review process. Discussions about strategic alternatives should be two-way communications in which good client ideas end up being pursued but where the client is convinced not to pursue courses that are likely to prove unhelpful.

Know when to make something a big issue with the government and when not to do so. There are some antitrust lawyers who seem to always want to pick fights with the government and others who never seem to perceive the need to do so. Neither of these approaches is optimal. There are times when being forceful is necessary and times when it is counterproductive. Know when to take either approach consistent with the client's interests. At all times, it is important for the antitrust lawyer and the client to maintain credibility with the government attorneys through fair dealing.

Keep in mind that not all deals are the same. For example, the approach to Second Request compliance and how quickly the issue in a merger investigation can be brought to a head may be very different where the client is a software company being acquired by a larger competitor that is losing key employees every day that the review continues than for a client that expects and can withstand a long review process.

Settling Merger Cases

In almost every merger, the goal is to convince the government not to bring a case challenging the transaction, rather than to win the case in court. Most merger investigations are resolved through the parties convincing the government that the apparent problems do not stand up to analysis. When that fails, the parties may offer to settle the investigation in a manner that satisfactorily addresses the government's concern but permits the transaction to proceed, normally with certain so-called curative divestitures. These settlements are embodied in consent decrees at both the FTC and DOJ.

There are a number of important strategies to successfully negotiating consent decrees with the federal antitrust authorities.

The consent decree negotiation process can take a relatively long time and delay consummation of a merger while it is ongoing. As a result, it is important that the antitrust lawyer and client communicate clearly from the outset so that the lawyer understands and can help the client to accomplish its strategic objectives. The lawyer needs to find out what the client is trying to accomplish, and to help the client weigh the consequences of delay in completing the deal against the costs of various parts of the potential settlement that the staff is seeking. The lawyer needs to identify objectively for the client what type of divestiture package clearly won't work and will cause delay if sought to be pursued as opposed to a package upon which there is a reasonable prospect of prevailing.

Protracted consent decree negotiations will delay consummation of the merger, deferring the attainment of synergies in the overall deal (not just the part that raises competitive problems). These synergies may be much more significant to the client than avoiding the divestiture of a few more assets to get the settlement completed sooner.

Be familiar with processes and practices employed at the FTC and DOJ respectively. While the approaches of the two agencies are broadly similar, there are real and important differences. For example, the FTC frequently requires an "up-front buyer" settlement, one that requires the parties to first find a buyer for the assets to be divested and enter into a contract for the divestiture so that the merger and the divestiture are completed contemporaneously or in close proximity. The DOJ rarely imposes a buyer up- front approach.

Understand the typical terms that the FTC or DOJ insist upon in their consent decrees – what is frequently referred to by agency staffs as the "boilerplate" in a consent decree. It is possible for parties to get bogged down arguing with staff on points that the reviewing agency is unlikely to change because the provision in question is the norm in many prior deals. Avoid fighting over terms that are not going to be changed by the agencies. Conversely, a good working knowledge of the normal consent decree provisions will allow you to know when the staff is overreaching so that you pick the right issues to fight on.

Litigating Merger Cases

Despite the best of efforts, there are cases in which the government cannot be convinced that the merger does not raise problems or should be allowed to proceed with divestitures. So there are merger cases in the US where it is necessary to litigate with the government.

Where the government is ready to litigate, the client has the option of settling (where acceptable terms can be reached), abandoning the deal, or litigating. From the defendant's standpoint, whether a merger case will settle or go to trial depends on a number of factors including the strategic importance of the merger at the time of litigation, the odds of prevailing against the government, and whether there is a contractual undertaking to litigate. The substantial cost of litigation can be an important factor. Antitrust merger cases are unavoidably expensive, involving substantial discovery conducted in a very short time frame, an expedited hearing, and substantial briefs and supporting papers. This is true to a substantial degree whether the deal is large or small. A company dealing with a $50 million deal may be adverse to spending several million dollars to litigate when that level of expense wouldn't cause as much concern in a much larger deal.

In recent years, the federal antitrust authorities have won most but not all of their merger cases. This is not terribly surprising. The government has a great deal of discretion that allows it to pick the cases to bring and to refrain from pursuing cases that do not look "winnable." Also, the agencies spend a great deal of time developing their litigation position during the merger review process so that by the time an investigation is completed they already may have witnesses and exhibits lined up for trial, while the parties haven't had access to a great deal of that information. For these and other reasons, the government should win most of its merger cases. However, there are times when the government chooses to litigate what ultimately proves not to be a very strong case.

Litigated merger cases in recent years tend to occur where there is a highly concentrated market and there are very few participants in the overall market. In the past decade, the FTC and DOJ have focused particularly on situations where the products or services offered by the merging parties are particularly close substitutes and there are arguably a very small number of close substitutes offered by third parties. In almost all recent litigated antitrust merger cases in the US, the government has characterized the merger as reducing the number of firms to whom a substantial set of customers can turn to a very small number (typically, from three to two), and contended that entry into the limited group of suppliers who can serve these customers is difficult.

Parties in litigated merger cases have responded to such arguments by contending that the government's view of the market is unduly narrow and ignores the fact that customers actually have many more than the three premerger choices identified by the government. When Office Depot and Staples sought to merge several years ago, the FTC argued that the market was limited to office supplies sold through office superstores, and that there were only three big players in that market. The parties countered that office supplies were sold through so many retail outlets that if the market were defined as the total retail sale of office supplies, there couldn't be an antitrust problem. The government prevailed because the district court was convinced that there was strong evidence (in the form of internal party documents, a book by Staple's founder, and econometric data) that office superstores priced lower than other retail outlets and only looked at other office superstores in setting their prices.

A different result was obtained two years ago, when the DOJ challenged a merger of two companies engaged in the disaster recovery business. These companies help corporations safeguard their information and computer systems in the event of a natural disaster or terrorist attack. The government argued there were only three companies in the market for providing remote disaster recovery sites that come into place when a corporation's system goes down. The defendants countered that while there were three companies who provide disaster recovery services in this particular manner, there were many other ways of doing disaster recovery. The parties argued that they actually competed with many third party vendors who did disaster recovery in other ways, and that they also competed against people doing it themselves. The court ultimately ruled for the defendants in what it described as a very close case.

The prospects for success in a merger case depend on many factors. Probably the most important is the identity of the federal district court judge who will decide the case. Federal judges have a great deal of discretion in determining the extent and form the preliminary injunction case will take including whether and to what extent there will be live testimony as opposed to written testimony and reliance on depositions and affidavits. The judge will decide how much pre-hearing discovery to allow, which can be critically important to the defendants who typically do not learn the identity of the government's witnesses until the litigation is commenced and who often seek third party discovery in order to provide a basis for cross-examination of the government's witnesses. The judge has considerable discretion to determine the duration of the proceeding, and the defense lawyers have important strategic decisions to make about how much time they want for the litigation. This frequently involves trade-offs between having more time to prepare the defense as against the benefits that may accrue in certain cases from holding the government's feet to the fire. Most important, an appeal of a federal district judge's decision to enjoin or deny an injunction in a government merger case is reviewed on an abuse of discretion standard, and given that many government cases that are litigated end up being close cases that could go either way, the trial judge's decision, if well thought out, is frequently considered unlikely to be reversed, and hence will often be the final decision in the case. One notable recent exception is the so-called baby food case in which the FTC lost its motion for a preliminary injunction blocking the merger of Heinz and Beechnut in the district court, but won the case on appeal in the D.C. Circuit.

Antitrust Reviews of Mergers and Acquisitions, Outside the United States

Globalization has had profound effects on the antitrust aspects of transactions. Over the past decade, I have been involved with increasing frequency in transactions reviewed by antitrust authorities outside the United States. This arises in several ways.

First, many transactions involve companies with operations in many countries. In addition to having to comply with the US antitrust laws, there are antitrust merger filing obligations in dozens of countries around the world. My colleagues and I advise companies on the issues initially, identifying which jurisdictions may require filings and whether there are likely to be serious substantive issues, and retain (or help the client to retain) local counsel in the appropriate jurisdictions. We work with local counsel to assure that the client's position is presented most effectively and in a manner that is not inconsistent with positions taken in other jurisdictions (unless justified by different market facts in the two jurisdictions, as sometimes happens). In transactions that are reviewed by multiple competition authorities, we normally serve as lead global antitrust counsel for the transaction, representing the client before the US agency and working with one or more foreign law firms on the merger review process abroad.

Second, I am consulted increasingly in deals that raise no US antitrust issues but may create concerns in jurisdictions abroad. I normally serve as the client's liaison with foreign antitrust counsel, helping to ensure that foreign counsel get the information and assistance they need in terms of filling out pre-merger notifications and presenting relevant facts to the competition authority. I am involved in determining the strategy and substantive arguments that are employed to get the deal through.

The EU is the foreign antitrust authority that I deal with most frequently. I have been involved in many EU pre-merger filings and a number of extensive investigations including two full merger review hearings conducted by DG-Competition, the staff of the European Commission in competition law matters. The EU antitrust pre-merger notification law, which is referred to as the Merger Regulation of the European Communities ("ECMR"), came into effect in 1991, and the EU authorities have been increasingly active in the merger area since.

If a proposed merger exceeds the relatively high worldwide and EU revenue thresholds established by the ECMR (basically, 5 billion euros in combined worldwide revenues and 250 million euros of EU revenues for each party, although there are lower alternative thresholds which are still substantial), then it is important from the outset to explain to the client the merger review process in the EU, which differs in a number of significant respects from the US merger review process. The EU employs a far more burdensome merger form than the US, and this form (referred to as "Form CO") is transaction specific, meaning that most of the information called for cannot be assembled in advance of any specific transaction, so that acquisition minded companies are not able to prepare a filing relatively quickly once a specific transaction is being pursued (the reverse is the case in the US). The EU staff reviews the extensive information provided in the Form CO and typically requires even more information before the filing is deemed sufficient and the timetables for the merger review begin to run. The EU process includes a "first phase" of review that is roughly analogous to the review conducted in the US in the first HSR waiting period, and then the EU determines whether the transaction should be subjected to a much more intense review in what is referred to as "second phase." If during the course of second phase, the deal continues to be viewed as problematic, the staff will issue a "statement of objections" (to which the parties may respond), and then will conduct a "hearing" at which the EU staff will lay out their concerns about the merger and then listen to presentations by the parties and interested third parties. Ultimately, the Commission will issue a final decision blocking the transaction or allowing it to proceed with or without remedies. There are provisions under the ECMR whereby the parties can offer remedies in either phase 1 or phase 2.

The EU process, like its counterpart in the US, is quite extensive and time consuming. There are, however, a number of important procedural differences with the US process.

First, the review is far less document and data intensive. Although the EU asks for a good deal of information from the parties, there is no analogue to the HSR Second Request.

Second, the tools that DG-Competition employs in its investigations are generally less intrusive than those employed by the FTC and DOJ. For example, the EU seeks information from parties and third parties principally through written requests (so-called "Article 11s") and doesn't employ the civil investigative demands for documents and sworn deposition testimony that are frequently used by the FTC and DOJ. Under reforms slated to go into effect in May 2004, the EU will acquire enhanced investigative powers in merger cases.

Third, the EU timetables are relatively certain. Once a filing is deemed sufficient to begin the process, which can take a month or in some cases even more, the EU Commission must decide the matter within first phase time period of roughly one month (25 working days effective May 2004) or trigger second phase, which must be completed within an additional period of about four months (90 working days effective May 2004).

Finally, the EU can block a transaction on its own, subject to judicial review that in the most expedited cases normally takes one to two years to complete. The transaction cannot be consummated prior to then. By contrast (and as noted above), the FTC or DOJ have no power to stop a transaction on their own, but instead must seek a preliminary injunction to block a deal.

I have been involved in extensive investigations by the antitrust authorities with a number of other foreign competition law authorities most notably in Canada, the United Kingdom, Australia and Venezuela. My colleagues and I have worked on merger review filings in dozens of other countries. Each country's enforcement authority is different, and one needs to work closely with local counsel to effectively represent the client's interests.

Significant Changes in Antitrust Law

A number of significant developments in recent times have changed the practice of antitrust law in mergers and acquisitions. These developments involve increased difficulty in completing mergers that are perceived at the outset as raising antitrust issues.

First, the US merger review process has become much more difficult to negotiate successfully and more adversarial. During the Clinton Administration, the agencies determined that they needed to do a better job in litigating merger cases, and as a result, they began to look to identify certain transactions as problematic from the start and to spend the investigation period building a litigation case. Prior to that time, while staffs were conscious that there might be litigation in the offing, they focused more of their investigation on determining whether to challenge, and at the end of the process scrambled to a greater degree to build their case. Now in conducting investigations, staff is seeking to identify and "pin down" witnesses with statements or testimony from early in the process. That makes it harder for lawyers trying to convince staffs not to bring a case. This approach appears to have continued in the second Bush Administration, and appears unlikely to change. The difficulty is exacerbated by the fact that competitors frequently retain antitrust counsel to bring concerns about mergers to the attention of the regulators. While such strategic behavior has always occurred to some degree, my impression is that organized opposition to mergers is more prevalent and merger opponents are more effective than in the past.

Second, it takes longer to resolve US merger investigations and the associated expenses have grown enormously. The amount of information that is reviewed in the process has expanded exponentially as a result of advances in information technology. There has been an explosion in the use of e-mail and electronic documents and data in corporations. With so much more information available, the government's desire to conduct a very thorough investigation means that literally gigabytes of data and hundreds (or in some cases thousands) of boxes of documents may have to be provided. Also, globalization has resulted in far more companies having offices and facilities abroad. Some companies now are truly international and multilingual, meaning that there is more occasion than ever before to produce documents that are written in a language other than English. In responding to Second Requests, the government takes the position that the parties must translate all documents in a language other than English. Translation of documents is very expensive and time consuming – translation in mergers can cost hundreds of thousands or even millions of dollars and take months to complete. Unless superiors at the FTC and DOJ are willing to limit staffs far more significantly than they have to date, this means that investigations will continue to grow in terms of length and costs to the parties. This problem is of concern in larger mergers, but is particularly problematic for small transactions, where the investigation costs are far more likely to be material in terms of the overall value of the deal.

Third, the federal antitrust agencies are not the only players in the antitrust process any more. During a period of relative inactivity by the federal agencies in the latter part of the Reagan Administration, state attorneys general began launching investigations of transactions and bringing actions to block mergers. The states have remained active in this area ever since, although they now tend in the first instance to work jointly with the federal authorities, who have been more welcoming of state participation since the first Bush Administration. State involvement further complicates efforts to complete mergers because state attorneys general frequently have more expansive enforcement agendas than the federal agencies.

Fourth, globalization has had a far more profound effect on antitrust M&A practice than simply increasing costs and expenses of the US process. The number of jurisdictions that merger parties have to address has multiplied significantly. When I left the DOJ and entered private practice over 20 years ago, the United States was the only country in the world that might block a merger on antitrust grounds before it was completed. That has changed completely. In the 1980s, Canada revised its competition laws and interposed a pre-merger notification requirement that has led to many filings and a substantial number of investigations. The EU adopted its Merger Regulation in the early 1990s, and it has successfully encouraged its member states to adopt their own merger control laws for transactions falling below the ECMR thresholds, so that most EU member states now have their own provisions. The demise of the Soviet Empire and Soviet Union - and the collapse of many authoritarian regimes that employed controlled economies (both of the political left and right) in many other parts of the world - led to the adoption of antitrust laws and frequently merger control provisions. Today, there are more than 70 countries that have pre-merger notification requirements in the Americas, Europe, South Africa, Israel and Asia (even China has adopted a merger control regime that applies to foreign companies and is working on a full set of antitrust laws).

The proliferation of merger control has created additional burdens. There are now many more filing requirements that have to be evaluated and many more filings that have to be made before a merger can be completed. There are more investigations, which means far higher transaction costs for completing mergers. It also means that there is a strong need for hiring antitrust counsel in several countries and having them coordinate their efforts to some degree, since the agencies are regularly working in tandem and sharing information in investigations, frequently pressuring parties into limited waivers of the confidentiality protections that would otherwise preclude such sharing of information among competition law agencies. There are now more jurisdictions that are capable of stopping a merger in its tracks prior to consummation, and even what have been widely regarded as "US transactions" have been stopped. In recent years, the EU stopped the GE/Honeywell merger and imposed significant conditions before allowing the Boeing/McDonald Douglas merger to proceed; conversely, the DOJ stopped the merger of the leading British and French industrial gas companies. Having more hurdles to clear means there is a greater risk that transactions will be stopped or that divestitures will be required that would not have occurred in the past.

In recent years, there have been efforts to address the various problems that I have noted. The FTC and DOJ has periodically announced "reforms" of the HSR process that result in more streamlined Second Requests and in procedures to avoid full investigations in appropriate cases through the limited initial investigation of potentially dispositive issues such as contentions that entry is easy. In the past, these efforts have resulted in some improvements at the margin, but far less than business and the antitrust bar have sought, and even the limited gains have proved transient. Antitrust enforcers have responded to concerns about the proliferation of merger control around the world through various initiatives which to date have had only limited private party input and have focused a great deal on improving antitrust enforcement techniques and seeking harmonization (certainly worthy goals) and much less on reducing burdens on merger parties.

Harmonization of Antitrust Laws around the World

There has been much concern expressed in the United States in recent years about inconsistent results in merger investigations. This is a problem, but one that is overstated, in my view.

Antitrust law is viewed as an important aspect of a nation's sovereignty and it is a way of protecting a country's own consumers from anticompetitive harm. As a result, antitrust authorities outside the United States are not going to rely on the US enforcement agencies to protect their consumers any more than the US agencies would rely on authorities outside the US to protect US consumer welfare. In the merger area, that creates potential for inconsistent results among jurisdictions.

Nevertheless, the similarities among the laws of most jurisdictions and among the major authorities like the EU and the US are much greater than the differences. Outcomes of merger investigations are normally consistent, and the divergences that occur are relatively rare and normally a function of different market facts in various countries – e.g., more significant overlaps with different entry conditions in one jurisdiction than in another. The antitrust authorities of both the US and the EU have noted frequently that they agree on outcomes far more frequently than they disagree, and they coordinate their investigations to minimize the likelihood of really divergent outcomes. When the EU or the US reaches different results on mergers that involve global markets, it is news precisely because it happens so infrequently.

To my mind, the more significant problem is that the proliferation of merger control provisions and antitrust laws in jurisdictions other than the US and EU has not always been accompanied by a fully developed appreciation of the role that antitrust should play in a market economy – that of being minimally intrusive so as to preclude artificial distortions of the competitive process without interfering with the competitive process itself. There have been remedies imposed by some antitrust enforcers in some parts of the world that would appear to be anti-competitive. There have been concerns and investigations that appear to have been prompted by political necessities or protectionist concerns, rather than competitive problems.

As I have noted, there are efforts underway at a number of different levels to promote greater understanding among antitrust enforcers of what is the appropriate analysis and to coalesce around a set of "best practices." Today, antitrust enforcers confer with each other frequently about specific investigations and general developments. These are important developments that should continue and intensify, since it is very unlikely that countries that do not presently have antitrust laws are going to refrain from adopting them when antitrust is perceived as one of the mainstays of a market economy.

The Future Direction of Antitrust Law

The analytic framework of antitrust law is well established. There are very few changes that occur in antitrust law. The Sherman Antitrust Act, the nation's first antitrust law, was adopted in 1890. To a large extent, there have not been major doctrinal changes in the case law in recent decades following the mid-1970s correction in course away from excess enforcement embodied in Supreme Court decisions such as General Dynamics in the merger area, GTE Sylvania as to vertical non-price restraints and BMI with regard to joint ventures. Much of the case law since then has been tinkering at the margin although there have been some significant cases more recently such as Liggett Group in predatory pricing cases.

The basic merger law, Section 7 of the Clayton Act, was adopted in 1914, amended very significantly in 1950, and has not been changed materially since. The most important statutory change in the ensuing half century has been the adoption of the HSR Act in 1976. That statue allows the government to challenge mergers before they are consummated, and thereby avoided the "scrambling of the eggs" problem that had plagued merger antitrust enforcement. In addition, the development of the DOJ/FTC horizontal merger guidelines, introduced in the first instance by Bill Baxter at the DOJ, was a profoundly important and positive doctrinal change. Following their adoption in 1981, the federal merger guidelines have been revised (mostly at the margin) three times in twenty-two years. There is broad consensus in the antitrust bar and among industrial organization economists that the guidelines have the analysis essentially right.

Some contend that we need new antitrust principles to deal with new industries. In my judgment, that argument is not well founded. To be sure, there are mergers that are reviewed today that involve industries that didn't exist five years ago. Antitrust laws are based on general principles that apply well to industries generally once the facts of the industry are well understood. Antitrust applies to all industries except for a relatively small number that are exempted by law – *e.g.*, insurance, securities to a certain extent. There are some industries that have had comparatively greater exposure to antitrust law because of cartel activities, a spate of mergers, or the presence of an allegedly dominant firm. But the courts in the US and the authorities both in the US and abroad are very suspicious of arguments that antitrust doesn't apply to a particular industry. Experience shows that for the most part, correctly dealing with new industries involves careful application of existing analysis to new fact situations.

For example, business-to-business networks became a major issue in antitrust laws a few years ago. Companies were entering into joint ventures that allowed for on-line trading with other companies or learning useful information, but there were antitrust issues because competitors were involved in the venture. I quickly formed the view that most of the issues could be identified and properly resolved using familiar concepts drawn from other types of joint venture activity based on older technologies. What was new about B2B exchanges was understanding the facts (*i.e.*, how the ventures worked). Once that was understood, the analysis for the most part was the same as had been applied to exchanges using less advanced technological means.

The real challenges in antitrust in the future are going to be applying the well-developed concepts to new industries. In the merger area, the analytical framework will likely stay generally the same (with some changes around the margins to reflect advances in economic theory), but it will be applied to factual situations that are impossible to predict today.

Michael Byowitz heads the antitrust department of Wachtell, Lipton, Rosen & Katz, focusing his practice on antitrust law and policy, and principally advising multinational corporations on major domestic and international mergers, acquisitions, joint ventures and corporate takeovers. He represents many clients before the Department of Justice and Federal Trade Commission in the United States and consults on investigations by foreign antitrust authorities in the European Union, Canada, Mexico, South America, Australia and many other jurisdictions. Before joining Wachtell, Lipton in 1983, Mr. Byowitz served as a Trial Attorney and Senior Trial Attorney with the US Department of Justice, Antitrust Division.

Mr. Byowitz is a leader of the American Bar Association's Section of International Law & Practice. He is presently the Section's Vice Chair (and will serve as Chair-Elect and Chair of the Section over the next two years); he is the former Chair of three of the Section's Divisions (General, Public International Law and Business Regulation) and is the former Chair of the Section's International Antitrust Law Committee. Mr. Byowitz has served as Chair of the Antitrust and Trade Regulation Committee of the Association of the Bar of the City of New York.

Mr. Byowitz writes articles on antitrust issues and is a contributor to legal publications, including two ABA books The International Lawyer's Desk Book and the Merger Review Process. He is a frequent speaker on international antitrust and compliance in the United States and abroad.

Mr. Byowitz received his AB from Columbia College in 1973 and his JD from New York University School of Law in 1976 (Order of the Coif).

Antitrust and Trade Regulation Law and Practice:

Managing Legal Risk to Facilitate Legitimate Competitive Business Activity

Robert T. Joseph

Partner

Sonnenschein Nath & Rosenthal LLP

The Fundamentals of Antitrust: What Are The Basic Features of the Antitrust Laws?

An appreciation for and understanding of the fundamentals of antitrust legal practice are, not surprisingly, facilitated by at least a basic grasp of what the antitrust laws are intended to prevent. While a thorough review of antitrust law and principles is not feasible here, an overview should be instructive and helpful.

Generally

The antitrust laws generally prohibit conduct -- either joint conduct pursuant to an agreement that unreasonably restrains trade, or anticompetitive exclusionary conduct by a firm that acquires or maintains monopoly power. An important body of antitrust law is aimed at *collusive conduct* (i.e., contracts, combinations or conspiracies) that have a substantial adverse effect on competition, because it raises prices or restricts output (e.g., an agreement among competitors to fix prices or allocate customers or geographic markets).

Other antitrust rules deal with *exclusionary* conduct that, by eliminating competitors from the market (or substantially impairing their ability to compete on the merits), allows or facilitates one or more remaining firms to exercise market power and thereby raise prices, restrict output or offer less variety to consumers.

The federal merger statute prohibits mergers or acquisitions that may tend to substantially lessen competition or create a monopoly in any line of commerce.

Brief Description of Key Antitrust Statutes
The four principal federal antitrust laws are the Sherman, Clayton, Robinson-Patman and Federal Trade Commission Acts. (Additionally, states have enacted antitrust laws patterned to varying degrees on these federal statutes, most often the Sherman Act.)

The Sherman Act. Contracts, combinations or conspiracies, i.e., agreements which unreasonably restrain trade or commerce are illegal under Section 1 of the Sherman Act. The courts have decided, for example, that *agreements between competitors* that fix prices; lead to production capacity curtailments; allocate territories or production; or constitute certain types of boycotts of third parties represent *per se* unreasonable restraint of trade and violate this section. Minimum resale price maintenance, i.e., an agreement between a supplier and a distributor as to the minimum resale price the distributor will resell the supplier's product, is also *per se* illegal.

Agreements are the basis of Section 1 antitrust violations. Unlike legitimate agreements or contracts, which in most instances must meet definite criteria before they are legally binding, illegal agreements can be found to exist under antitrust law without being formalized or explicit. And while commercial agreements must have clarity, no such clarity is required for an agreement in violation of the antitrust laws. An illegal agreement may be inferred from circumstantial evidence in the form of conduct.

It is important to recognize that certain activities are so injurious to competition, while at the same time are so unlikely to have any pro-competitive benefits, that they are not only termed anticompetitive *per se*, but also may well be punished by criminal sanctions. These activities include bid-rigging, price-fixing and market allocation. There is no defense to such violations of antitrust law; no explanations or justifications are entertained by the courts.

Under Section 2 of the Sherman Act, it is illegal for any person to monopolize, attempt to monopolize, or to join or conspire with others to monopolize, any part of trade or commerce. In general, this section prohibits the possession of power to control prices or access to the market if such power was obtained or used with intent to monopolize. It is not illegal to acquire monopoly power through superior products or skills or even through luck. What is prohibited is acquiring, or attempting to acquire, or maintaining monopoly power through unfair and unreasonably exclusive tactics. An example of an attempt to monopolize would be price- cutting below costs with intent to drive competitors out of business and secure a monopoly position, when it is likely that the price-cutting firm can "recoup" its losses from the price-cutting by making greater than normal profits after its competitors have left the market.

The Sherman Act is applicable to all transactions, regardless of where they occurred, that have any substantial effect on the domestic trade and imports into the United States. The Sherman Act also applies to U.S. export trade if the activity has a direct, substantial, and reasonably foreseeable effect on such export trade.

Serious violations of Section 1 of the Sherman Act (such as price-fixing or market allocation among competitors or bid-rigging) may be the subject of criminal actions brought by the Department of Justice. Prison sentences of up to three years can be imposed on individual employees convicted of criminal offenses. These offenses are categorized as felonies. A fine of up to $10,000,000 against a corporation and up to $350,000 against an individual may be levied for each criminal offense, and defendants may be subject to greater fines equal to twice the gain to them from their illegal conduct or twice the loss to the victims of the offense.

There has been a dramatic surge of cartel enforcement activity in the last decade. A very important factor contributing to this growth has been the adoption by the United States of its amnesty program and by similar programs in other key jurisdictions active in anti-cartel efforts. The U.S. Department of Justice's Corporate Leniency Policy, initiated in 1978, was changed to provide additional incentives for companies to come forward and cooperate. Major features of the revised program included automatic amnesty, post-investigation amnesty and complete protection for cooperating individuals. The revised policy had an enormous impact on criminal antitrust enforcement in the United States, generating a significant number of new and frequently large cases, especially in the international cartel area, in turn resulting in huge increases in the size of financial penalties imposed on companies and individuals and in the number and length of prison sentences for individuals convicted of antitrust offenses.

Non-criminal actions can be brought by the Department of Justice to seek injunctive relief to stop and prevent conduct illegal under the antitrust laws.

The Clayton Act. Section 3 of this Act concerns the sale or lease of commodities where competition is substantially lessened through abusive exclusive dealing, tying and full-line forcing, arrangements and certain requirements contracts.

Section 7 of the Clayton Act is the federal merger statute that, as noted above, prohibits mergers and acquisitions that may substantially lessen competition or tend to create a monopoly in a line of commerce. The unifying theme of merger law is that mergers should not be permitted to create or enhance market power or to facilitate its exercise. In analyzing whether to challenge a horizontal merger between competitors, the federal agency analyzing the merger (the Department of Justice or the

Federal Trade Commission) will first assess whether the merger would significantly increase concentration and result in a concentrated market, properly defined and measured. Second, the agency assesses whether the merger, in light of market concentration and other factors that characterize the market, raises concern about potential adverse competitive effects. Third, the agency assesses whether entry would be timely, likely and sufficient either to deter or counteract the competitive effects of concern. Fourth, the agency assesses any efficiency gains that reasonably cannot be achieved by the parties through other means. Finally, the agency assesses whether, but for the merger, either party to the transaction would be likely to fail, causing its assets to exit the market. The process of assessing market concentration, potential adverse competitive effects, entry, efficiency and failure is a tool that allows the agency to answer the ultimate inquiry in merger analysis: whether the merger is likely to create or enhance market power or to facilitate its exercise.

The Robinson-Patman Act. Among other things, this technical, complex and often confusing Act prohibits charging different prices for the same product to customers who are in competition with each other, where the price differential may cause an adverse effect on competition among the customers or with competing suppliers, unless the difference in price is cost-justified, was offered in good faith to meet lower prices, or meets other defenses. As a customer, a buyer cannot knowingly induce or receive an illegal price differential. This Act also prohibits offering promotional payments, services or assistance on a disproportionate basis to competing purchasers of the same product unless the offer is made to meet competitive offers.

The Federal Trade Commission Act. Section 5 of this Act, which is enforced by an administrative agency, the Federal Trade Commission, bars unfair methods of competition and unfair or deceptive acts or practices, including false or misleading advertising, false disparagement of competitors or their products, use of lottery devices, and commercial bribery. Violations of the antitrust laws (such as Sections 1 and 2 of the Sherman Act) are also "unfair methods of competition" that violate the Federal Trade Commission Act and may be the subject of an action by the Commission.

Various Remedies. In addition to the criminal penalties and governmental actions described above, persons or firms whose businesses are damaged may recover in civil suits three times the amount of their damages plus attorneys' fees, and all other costs of litigation. Class actions have been brought on behalf of purchasers of products or services claimed to have been injured by price-fixing and on behalf of persons otherwise believed to have been injured by antitrust violations. Federal courts may issue injunctions aimed at preventing illegal conduct and restoring competition, and the Federal Trade Commission may cease and desist orders of the same nature, which may contain prohibitions going beyond the scope of the violation originally involved.

Non-U.S. Antitrust Laws. Antitrust laws that prohibit many of the same activities prohibited in the United States are in effect in numerous countries, including virtually all major commercial countries, and careful consideration must be given to the applicable laws of all jurisdictions in which a transaction possibly involving a competitive restraint is to take place.

The chief antitrust regime outside the United States is found in the Rome Treaty of 1957, which established the European Common Market ("Common Market"). Article 85(1) of the Treaty specifically prohibits all agreements and concerted practices that are likely to affect trade between the member states and that have as their object or result the prevention, restriction, or distortion of competition within the European

Union. Examples deemed to fall within Article 85(1) include such restraints as price-fixing, production limitation, unjustified price discrimination, and tie-in arrangements. Article 85(3) allows the Commission of the European Communities to exempt from the prohibition of Article 85(1) agreements which may be shown to contribute toward improving production or distribution of goods or promoting technical or economic progress within the Common Market while reserving to users a fair share in the profit without (a) imposing upon the enterprises concerned any restriction that is not essential to attaining such objectives, or (b) giving such firms the power to eliminate competition in a substantial part of the Common Market. Article 86 prohibits the misuse of dominant market positions.

One of the actions that may be taken by the Commission of the European Communities, in the event of violation, is the imposition of a fine. The Commission regularly imposes substantial fines in cases involving agreements between competitors adopting concerted practices, including price-fixing and in cases involving misuse of dominant market positions. The fines have been levied against parties headquartered both inside and outside the Common Market.

What Are The Fundamentals of an Antitrust Expert's Practice?

This admittedly brief description of key antitrust laws points to the roles of the antitrust legal expert. The fundamental tasks of this specialist include (a) helping the client understand the nature and scope of the antitrust laws and potential consequences for failing to comply with them (e.g., including the criminal penalties, government civil actions, and private actions by consumers or competitors, which are described above); (b) exploring with the client which antitrust statutes or rules have or are likely to have the most impact on the client's business; (c) working with the client in formulating a compliance program and rules of conduct designed to avoid or minimize antitrust risk, particularly with respect to antitrust violations that may carry criminal penalties; (d) identifying and assessing the antitrust law risks and consequences of proposed business and marketing strategies and, where appropriate, exploring with the client alternative courses of action that satisfy legitimate business objectives while minimizing antitrust risks.

Because certain antitrust violations (e.g., agreements to fix prices, divide or allocate markets or customers, or rig bids) are very serious, and in the United States (and, increasingly, in other countries as well) can be prosecuted criminally, antitrust counselors may be involved in educating the client to make sure that its executives understand the consequences of behavior subject to criminal prosecution and advising the client as it implements rules for corporate compliance. This involves (a) emphasizing with corporate employees the principle that, as a general matter, conduct of the business vis-à-vis competitors must be based on independent business judgment and that, because the client competes vigorously on the basis of price, quality and service, it needs to acquire in legitimate ways information about its competitors' strategies and their efforts to obtain the business of customers and potential customers, and (b) emphasizing with corporate employees the need to avoid conduct involving competitors, customers or suppliers suggesting that an illegal agreement exists.

Other business activity may raise significant antitrust issues or questions, but yet not be of a type for which criminal sanctions are typically sought. Not infrequently business conduct (such as an acquisition of, or joint venture with, a competitor; agreements obligating customers to purchase all of their needs from the client-seller; and charging different prices for the same product to competing customers) may fall into a "gray area" of legality. In such circumstances, whether or not a company complies with the antitrust laws may be unclear, may turn on the underlying facts peculiar to the parties and business involved, and may involve legal principles or rules whose impact and meaning are unsettled.

Antitrust advisors sometimes counsel clients about a business opportunity, project or initiative that may not be either clearly legal or clearly illegal, but that could, depending on the factual situation, raise significant antitrust legal risk. The antitrust counselor applies (a) his or her knowledge of the governing legal principles and judicial interpretation of those principles, (b) to the facts that counselor knows from experience and legal precedent control or in a major way affect the legal analysis.

The relevant facts often involve, for example, the product and geographic markets in which the client competes, the degree to which it has market power (an inquiry that in turn implicates consideration such as the definition of the market in which it competes and barriers to entry or effective competition in the market); the likely impact of the restraint on prices and output; and the business reasons for which the practice is being undertaken. The counselor will then assess for the client the degree of antitrust risk involved in light of the legal rules and relevant factors. As just noted, the counselor may also explore with the client alternative ways to structure the transaction or practice in order to minimize, and even substantially reduce, antitrust risk, while at the same time achieving the client's business objectives.

The key skills that an antitrust lawyer can bring to the table for the benefit of the client include, of course, an in-depth knowledge and appreciation of antitrust law and its objectives, rules and principles. An antitrust expert should have an understanding and appreciation for those economic disciplines (such as microeconomics and industrial organization) that have increasingly become imbedded in antitrust analysis. An antitrust lawyer should be prepared, indeed eager, to understand a number of dimensions of the client's business, such as business objectives and strategies, the competitive milieu in which it operates, and its corporate values and culture.

An antitrust counselor is best equipped to advise clients (or litigate antitrust claims on their behalf) when proceeding from her or his own accumulated personal counseling or litigation experience, supplemented by the experience of other antitrust experts in his or her firm. (This includes an awareness of current and anticipated government enforcement policy, embodied in current prosecutorial initiatives, speeches and policy statements, and personal experience with agencies.) Drawing on this experience, the skilled counselor is able to think through how particular conduct will be viewed by a jury, judge or government agency in assessing antitrust risk and should be able to explain to the client simply and directly why certain types of conduct will or will not be viewed with suspicion, e.g., "Here is how what you want to do may well be viewed by a judge or jury. . . ." This storehouse of knowledge and experience enables the antitrust counselor to better identify and explain practical risk and to explore and identify alternatives for structuring a transaction or course of conduct, so that the conduct will not give rise to a misleading impression of impropriety to persons (e.g., jurors) who are not intimately involved in the client's business on a daily basis.

Top-notch antitrust counselors will have a strong intellectual interest in antitrust law, economics and policy. This intellectual curiosity often has a strong practical payoff because it helps the lawyer identify cutting-edge issues and, more generally, to think creatively when approaching difficult antitrust issues of critical importance to the client. In short, the degree to which an antitrust lawyer has an intellectual curiosity in the subject matter, blended with a keen interest (even fascination) with the client's business and the transaction being analyzed, and an eagerness to work with the client to explore ways in which to minimize antitrust risk, often distinguishes that practitioner from others.

The Art of the Antitrust Counselor: Strategies or Methodologies

When approaching an antitrust case, as the foregoing indicates, the counselor seeks to understand the client's business objectives (which often involve having a firm grasp of manufacturing, marketing and financial facts relating to that client). It is an intrinsic part of antitrust counseling to determine the pro-competitive reason for a transaction or business conduct, including how it may ultimately benefit consumers (by, e.g., improving product quality, lowering costs, lowering prices, leading to more effective or expanded distribution). Antitrust principles are always applied in the context of a particular situation, so it is helpful to understand the client's specific industry and market.

In industries where there are only a few sellers collectively holding a large market share, the antitrust expert may be asked to help ensure that the client does not engage in conduct suggesting (accurately or not) that the firms in that industry are engaged in collusive or exclusionary conduct. Having a large market share or being in an industry with a few sellers by itself is not illegal. But these conditions often present a situation in which the client should exercise particular care, and in certain situations the legality of a particular business strategy may turn on whether the seller-client has substantial market power.

The Structure of Antitrust Analysis: An Example

Because of the extensive variety of business practices and their settings, it is difficult to select a particular "example" that fully captures the craft of the antitrust lawyer. An example that might provide a useful glimpse at how an antitrust expert approaches a proposed course of conduct involves a common form of business enterprise -- joint ventures. How might an antitrust expert approach the antitrust law consequences of a joint venture that a client wishes to enter into with one of its competitors to develop a new product?

The antitrust counselor would assess whether the joint venture contained agreements not to compete on price, output or customers that are not reasonably related to the integration contemplated by the joint venture or reasonably necessary to achieve the venture's procompetitive benefits, so that "*per se* illegality" issues might be raised with respect to those provisions. If there is a significant question whether the agreements or provisions are not reasonably related or reasonably necessary, the antitrust advisor might want to explore the feasibility and workability of less restrictive options in order to minimize or eliminate antitrust risk.

If such restrictions do not raise "*per se* illegality" issues, procompetitive benefits, the counselor would then consider whether the joint venture's various provisions nonetheless unreasonably restrained trade under a "rule of reason" analysis, by focusing on the state of competition with, as compared to without, the joint venture and its various provisions, in an effort to determine whether the joint venture agreement would likely harm competition by increasing the ability or incentive profitably to raise prices or reduce output, quality, service, or innovation below what likely would prevail in the absence of the agreement and its provisions.

This "rule of reason approach" would involve a close examination of the proposed terms of the joint venture and their functions, an understanding of the businesses of the parties and of the relevant industry, including how the relevant market would be defined in light of commercial realities and applicable law, the identities of market participants, the market positions (i.e., shares of the market) accounted for the parties to the venture and others in the market, the barriers to entry and effective competition in the market, and the number and strength of other actual or potential sellers in the relevant product market in the market before and after the joint venture is formed and operating.

The purpose of the venture would be examined. For example, the parties may be interested in a joint venture because they have complementary assets or skills and believe that by bringing them together they will be able to better develop or manufacture a new product than if proceeding alone. These objectives would point to the legitimacy of the joint venture and can be referred to in justifying various undertakings and commitments that might otherwise be viewed with some suspicion.

In terms of dealing with government agencies, the counselor would determine whether this particular joint venture is reportable under the Hart Scott-Rodino Act, depending on its size, the size of the parties and the structure of the transaction. The counselor would plan with the lawyers representing the other party to the joint venture the best strategy for dealing with any significant foreseeable antitrust issues to the government agency that would be looking at it. Counsel would determine whether the customers of the companies would react favorably to the joint venture and, in that regard, may at an appropriate time wish to alert their customers about the transaction and explain why the proposed transaction makes sense from the customers' viewpoint. Depending on the level of risk and the seriousness of the antitrust issues, antitrust counsel might consider retaining an economist who could offer advice in a consulting capacity with respect to any issues that arise. The antitrust team would assess and analyze (revising as the process continues) what arguments and facts should be marshaled to present to government agencies to persuade them that no enforcement action (or even an extensive investigation) is necessary or appropriate.

Counsel will want to guide the parties not to take any actions prior to the transaction's closing that could be viewed as coordinating or carrying out the enterprise before the Hart-Scott-Rodino Act waiting requirements are met.

Clients – Risks, Misconceptions and Key Advice

The preceding suggests considerations to be considered or evaluated in identifying, assessing and minimizing antitrust risk:

1.   Because of the serious consequences flowing from *per se* illegal conduct in the form of price-fixing, bid rigging and market or customer allocation, the counselor must assess whether conduct that is proposed, or detected, may not only be illegal, but also criminal in nature. If the conduct is illegal, the client must be advised against it, most especially when criminal penalties may be attached. (Detection of criminal activity raises significant issues of whether to seek amnesty under the Department of Justice amnesty program and that of other jurisdictions.)

2.   More generally, risk assessment is shaped by evaluation of a number of interrelated considerations. They include: (a) the market shares (in properly-defined antitrust "relevant markets") of the parties to arrangements or agreements; (b) whether the arrangement is one between competitors (horizontal) or between a supplier and its distributor (vertical), the former viewed with more suspicion than the latter (except for minimum resale price-fixing, which is a *per se* illegal vertical restraint); (c) the effect of the conduct on the competitive process, and the extent

to which that conduct suggests that its real purpose is to raise prices or restrict output rather than to increase output, reduce costs or offer more efficiencies. The impact a particular practice will have on competitors or customers (who may be potential private action plaintiffs) may also be assessed. Conduct likely to have a devastating effect on a competitor or customer (such as driving it out of business) may present greater risks. However, probable deleterious impact on competitors or customers does not mean that the course of action is illegal, or even that the client should not go forward with it. Rather it is a factor that should be evaluated in making risk assessments, especially bearing on the probability of litigation

3.   It is important for the client to appreciate that the Hart Scott-Rodino Act filing and any subsequent investigation in connection with a merger or joint venture can potentially affect the timing of the closing of a reportable transaction. If the timing is affected, such delays may affect the transaction's financing, strategy and integration. (Timing may be further complicated if premerger filings are required in the European Union and other foreign jurisdictions, with their own filing requirements, waiting periods and potential agency inquiries.) In addition, if there is an extensive investigation by an agency, there could be a significant amount of assistance required from the client's executives, not only in helping develop a presentation of facts in favor of the transaction, but also in terms of working on a day-to-day basis with the lawyers as the strategies unfold. Unless clients have been through the exercise before (many have), executives may be surprised by the intensity and depth of a government investigation, involving a significant amount of document production and even deposition testimony (particularly if there is a request for additional information (a "second request") in the United States). Therefore, the client needs to understand that processes or procedures need to be in place to facilitate the production of required information to government agencies. Agencies in the United States have

issued statements and policies concerning procedures that may be followed in order to expedite more extensive reviews and to do so with minimized expense.

4.   Some companies, particularly smaller firms, may confuse firm size with antitrust vulnerability. They may mistakenly believe that antitrust enforcement is only concerned with firms whose annual sales volumes are very large, and cannot understand why there is an interest by the government in their particular merger transaction or in the pricing practices or other conduct of firms in their industry, when the government did not previously challenge very large merger transactions or investigate firms in large and prominent industries. However, government agencies' interest in a transaction is not determined by how large (dollar size or assets) the companies are, but rather by their position in the market (e.g., their market share, even in a relatively small overall market), or by the type of conduct involved (e.g., price fixing or market allocation). For example, price-fixing or bid-rigging cases may be brought against firms with relatively small sales in absolute dollars, even selling in small, local markets, because price-fixing is viewed as a very serious offense. It is no defense that the price-fixing or bid-rigging does not involve many consumers (compared to other industries), because conspiracies of these types are considered to be serious offenses with no redeeming value. The agencies believe that it is their job is to protect competition from illegal conduct, even in "small" markets with firms whose sales are much smaller than Fortune 500 firms.

5.   Many firms have an antitrust compliance program tailored to their specific needs. The most successful programs consist of a written policy with appropriate supplementary instruction and monitoring. Antitrust counsel can assist in developing such a policy.

6.   Many antitrust specialists not only counsel clients on the antitrust implications of business conduct, but also litigate antitrust cases. Antitrust litigation tends to be expensive and complicated, characterized by extensive pre-trial discovery (often including production of massive amounts of business documents to one's adversary and depositions of corporate employees), use of expert consultants and witnesses (including economic and accounting experts who testify on market-related and damage issues), and protracted time frames. Antitrust specialists who also litigate antitrust cases are able to use their litigation experience in counseling clients concerning the litigation risks of particular courses of action.

Some Current and Emerging Trends and Areas of Interest

1.   Increasingly over the last fifteen years a number of countries have adopted some form of antitrust or "competition" law. Presently more than 100 nations have competition laws, and over 60 have merger control rules. U.S. agencies cooperate closely with various other enforcement authorities with the governments of other countries (including those of the European Union, Canada, Japan and Mexico) in investigating cartels and other anticompetitive behavior. This combination of increased antitrust enforcement abroad and inter-governmental cooperation points to the need for antitrust compliance efforts and sensitivity cooperation can be expected to increase in the future; it means that companies, particularly those who market internationally, will have to even be more vigilant about their antitrust compliance.

There is currently no international antitrust "code" binding on all or some group of nations. However, with increased dialogue and cooperation among antitrust authorities, many believe that enforcers in different countries will "converge" in some substantial ways in their approaches to antitrust theory, policy, enforcement and investigative techniques.

2.   Experienced antitrust counselors in the U.S. monitor developments in the international arena and keep clients abreast of major developments abroad that may affect them.   Many major U.S. corporations have antitrust attorneys familiar with international issues. Developing antitrust compliance programs that embrace international operations is a current challenge for firms with global activities.

3.   Detection and punishment of international price-fixing cartels has been an increasing emphasis of U.S enforcers and other countries as well, and that trend can be expected to continue. Governmental cartel actions are inevitably followed by private class actions brought on behalf of direct purchasers (under federal law) and indirect purchasers (under the law of many states). These private actions, which may be brought by many plaintiffs and States in federal and state courts, can be enormously expensive in terms of potential risk of liability and in terms of costs of defense and disruption to the businesses of defendants.   Private actions outside the U.S., brought in foreign courts and under foreign law, on behalf of citizens in other countries harmed by price-fixing and other cartel behavior, may well place a greater role on the antitrust enforcement scene. Criminal international cartel investigations may well play a number of other issues, including whether to seek amnesty under the amnesty programs of the Department of Justice and foreign competition law authorities.

4.   While certain conduct (such as horizontal price- fixing, horizontal market and customer allocation, certain boycotts, and vertical minimum resale price-fixing) is *per se* illegal, over the last twenty-five years courts and agencies have developed a more refined analysis of and a

more cautious approach to defining what conduct should be considered *per se* illegal. Antitrust "rule of reason" analysis is also more sophisticated, with courts and counsel considering when it is appropriate to apply a "truncated" or "abbreviated" determination that a practice unreasonably restrains trade.

5.   With the expanded emphasis on cartel behavior, particularly international cartels, with strong policy statements from U.S. agencies on the need for timely, effective relief in merger cases (litigated or settled by consent), and with debate over the role of the private action and, in particular, the treble damages remedy and the class action device in the remedies system, continuing debate over antitrust remedies can be expected.

6.   Considerable attention has been given to the question of whether antitrust rules should be different or applied in some significantly different way in so-called "high technology" industries, where intellectual property is often the source of competitive advantage; where "network effects" may be significant; where cooperation among competitors may lead to standards that promote and ultimately lead to substantial benefits to consumers; and where markets often rapidly develop and are eclipsed. The intersection of antitrust law and intellectual property law, including the extent to which these bodies of legal doctrine are in conflict or really are complementary, is a related subject that has spawned much debate and discussion. Future cases can be expected to address these questions.

Mr. Joseph has extensive experience in the litigation and counseling of antitrust, trade regulation and franchising matters. The issues in these matters have frequently been complex, and they have covered a wide variety of substantive law issues and procedural litigation questions. He has also handled other commercial litigation issues and matters. Mr. Joseph's antitrust experience has involved cases and counseling with respect to all of the major antitrust laws and the subjects within them. He has participated in a number of antitrust cases encompassing distribution issues for McDonald's Corporation and other clients. He has been actively involved in major cases alleging price fixing, such as the Corrugated Container Antitrust litigation and the Glass Containers litigation.

In addition to his just-completed term as Chair of the American Bar Association Antitrust Law Section, Mr. Joseph previously served as the Section's Chair-Elect and Vice-Chair, and as Committee Officer on the Section's Council, and as Chair of its Franchising Committee (1984-1987), Chair of its Videotapes Committee (1987-1990), and Chair of its Publications Committee (1991-1994). He also was Vice Chair of the Franchising Committee (1981-1984) and of the Publications Committee (1990-1991).

Prior to joining the Sonnenschein firm, Mr. Joseph was a staff attorney from 1971 to 1976 in the headquarters office of the Federal Trade Commission's Bureau of Competition. He also served as the assistant to the director of the Bureau of Competition in 1973-74.

Mr. Joseph served as a member of the Archdiocesan Pastoral Council of the Archdiocese of Chicago, a consultative body to the Archbishop of Chicago. He served as a Trustee of the Northbrook Public Library from 1979 to 1989, was its president from 1983 to 1985, and served in various other officer positions.

He graduated from the University of Michigan where he received his JD, cum laude, in 1971. He was a member of the Michigan Law Review, Alpha Sigma Nu, National Honor Society. He graduated from Xavier University with his AB, magna cum laude, in 1968.

Executive Reports

Targeted Reports Featuring Hundreds of C-Level Perspectives

Executive Reports: How to Get an Edge as a Lawyer

This insider look at the legal profession is written by current chairs/managing partners from over 100 of the top 200 largest law firms. Each senior partner shares their knowledge on how to get an edge as a lawyer, from time management to negotiation tactics to ways to manage expectations with your clients. Also covered are over 250 specific, proven innovative legal strategies and methodologies practiced by the leading attorneys of the world that have helped them gain an edge. This report is designed to give you insight into the leading lawyers of the world, and assist you in developing additional "special skills" that can help you be even more successful as a lawyer.

$279 – 70 Pages, 8.5 x 11

Executive Reports: The Lawyer's Industry Guide for Client Acquisition & Retention

This insider look at over 30 major industries and professions, written by over 200 C-Level executives is ideal for landing new clients, keeping up to speed on a wide variety of industries, and when you need to "get smart fast" on a particular topic. Each industry overview has sections written by current, leading C-Level executives (CEOs, CFOs, CTOs, CMOs, Partners) from companies such as GE, Coke, Amex, Duke Energy and other blue chip companies from every major industry that enables you to speak intelligently with anyone after being "briefed" by a leading executive from that industry.

$549 - 560 Pages, 8.5x11

Legal Books

Visit Your Local Bookseller Today or www.Aspatore.com For More Information

- Inside the Minds: Leading Lawyers - Managing Partners From Akin Gump, King & Spaulding, Morrison & Foerster and More on the Art & Science of Being a Successful Lawyer, 240 Pages, $37.95
- Inside the Minds: Leading Litigators - Litigation Chairs From Weil Gotshal & Manges, Jones Day, Paul Weiss and More on the Art & Science of Litigation, 240 Pages, $37.95
- Inside the Minds: Leading Intellectual Property Lawyers - IP Chairs From Foley & Lardner, Blank Rome, Hogan & Hartson & More on the Art & Science of Intellectual Property Law, 240 Pages, $37.95
- Inside the Minds: Leading Labor Lawyers - Labor/Employment Chairs From Thelen Reid & Pries, Wilson Sonsini, Perkins Coie & More on the Art & Science of Labor & Employment Law, 240 Pages, $37.95
- Inside the Minds: Leading Product Liability Lawyers - Product Liability Chairs From Debevoise & Plimpton, Kaye Scholer, Bryan Cave and More on the Art & Science Behind a Successful Product Liability Practice, 240 Pages, $37.95
- International Product Liability Law: A Worldwide Desk Reference Featuring Product Liability Laws & Procedures For Over 60 Countries, 1020 Pages, $219.95
- Inside the Minds: The Art & Science of Bankruptcy Law - Bankruptcy Chairs from Perkins Coie, Reed Smith, Ropes & Grey and More on Successful Strategies for Bankruptcy Proceedings, 240 Pages, $37.95
- Inside the Minds: The Corporate Lawyer - Corporate Chairs From Dewey Ballantine, Holland & Knight, Wolf Block & More on Successful Strategies for Business Law, 240 Pages, $37.95
- Inside the Minds: Firm Leadership - Managing Partners From Dykema Gossett, Thatcher Proffitt & Wood and More on the Art & Science of Managing a Law Firm, 240 Pages, $37.95
- Inside the Minds: Leading Deal Makers - Leading VC's and Lawyers Share Their Knowledge on Negotiations, Leveraging Your Position and the Art of Deal Making, 240 Pages, $37.95
- Inside the Minds: The Innovative Lawyer - Managing Partners From Bryan Cave, Jenner & Block, Buchanan Ingersoll & More on Becoming a Senior Partner in Your Firm, 240 Pages, $37.95

Buy All 11 Legal Books for Your Library
Save 50% – Only $349 (Includes S&H)
Call 1-866-Aspatore (277-2867) to Order

Other Best Sellers

Visit Your Local Bookseller Today or www.Aspatore.com For A Complete Title List

- <u>Term Sheets & Valuations</u> – A Line by Line Look at the Intricacies of Term Sheets & Valuations, 100 Pages, $14.95

- <u>Deal Terms</u> – The Finer Points of Deal Structures, Valuations, Term Sheets, Stock Options and Getting Deals Done, 240 Pages, $49.95

- <u>Inside the Minds: The Ways of the VC</u> - VCs from Polaris, Bessemer, Venrock, Mellon Ventures & More on Identifying Opportunities, Assessing Business Models & Establishing Valuations, 220 Pages, $27.95

- <u>The Golf Course Locator for Business Professionals</u> – Golf Courses Closest to Largest Companies, Law Firms, Cities & Airports, 180 Pages, $12.95

- <u>Business Travel Bible</u> – Must Have Phone Numbers, Business Resources & Maps, 240 Pages, $14.95

- <u>Living Longer, Working Stronger</u> – Simple Steps for Business Professionals to Capitalize on Better Health, 160 Pages, $14.95

- <u>Business Grammar, Style & Usage</u> – Rules for Articulate and Polished Business Writing and Speaking, 100 Pages, $14.95

- <u>ExecRecs</u> – Executive Recommendations For The Best Business Products & Services, 140 Pages, $14.95

- <u>Executive Adventures</u> – 50+ Exhilarating Out of the Office Escape Vacations, 100 Pages, $14.95

- <u>The C-Level Test</u> – Business IQ & Personality Test for Professionals of All Levels, 60 Pages, $17.95

- <u>The Business Translator</u> – Business Words, Phrases & Customs in Over 65 Languages, 540 Pages, $29.95